FIVE NIGHTS
IN
Paris

ALSO BY JOHN BAXTER

Paris at the End of the World

The Perfect Meal

*The Most Beautiful Walk
in the World*

Von Sternberg

Carnal Knowledge

Immoveable Feast

We'll Always Have Paris

A Pound of Paper

Science Fiction in the Cinema

Buñuel

Fellini

Stanley Kubrick

Steven Spielberg

Woody Allen

George Lucas

De Niro

TRANSLATED BY JOHN BAXTER

My Lady Opium by Claude Farrère

Morphine by Jean-Louis Dubut de Laforest

The Diary of a Chambermaid by Octave Mirbeau

Gamiani, or Two Nights of Excess by Alfred de Musset

FIVE NIGHTS

IN

Paris

After Dark in the City of Light

JOHN BAXTER

HARPER ● PERENNIAL

NEW YORK ● LONDON ● TORONTO ● SYDNEY ● NEW DELHI ● AUCKLAND

HARPER PERENNIAL

FIVE NIGHTS IN PARIS. Copyright © 2015 by John Baxter. All rights reserved. Printed in the United States of America. No part of this book may be used or reproduced in any manner whatsoever without written permission except in the case of brief quotations embodied in critical articles and reviews. For information address HarperCollins Publishers, 195 Broadway, New York, NY 10007.

HarperCollins books may be purchased for educational, business, or sales promotional use. For information please e-mail the Special Markets Department at SPsales@harpercollins.com.

FIRST EDITION

Library of Congress Cataloging-in-Publication Data is available upon request.

ISBN 978-0-06-229625-2

15 16 17 18 19   OV/RRD   10 9 8 7 6 5 4 3 2 1

Contents

PROLOGUE:
THE DANGEROUS EDGE   1

1. AS THROUGH A GLASS,
   AND DARKLY   5
2. WOODY'S NIGHTS   9
3. UNDER COVER   17
4. THE DARK SIDE   22
5. PROMENADES   26
6. FIVE LADIES FEELING   34
7. THE RIGHT WAY TO WRITE   39
8. WHITE NIGHTS   45
9. NOISES AT NIGHT   53

Contents

Night 1: Sound

10.	BLUES IN THE NIGHT	65
11.	PARIS ON SEA	72
12.	RASPBERRY AND ROSE PETALS	76
13.	EATING WELL IS THE BEST REVENGE	83
14.	TIME AND TIDE	87
15.	SPENDING A CENTIME	93
16.	HELP THE POOR STRUGGLER	103
17.	THE SENSE OF A SACRIFICE	110
18.	BEHIND CLOSED DOORS	122
19.	LOVE AND FRESH WATER	129

Night 2: Taste

20.	POOR FOOD?	141
21.	STRICTLY FROM HUNGER	147
22.	PROPOSING A TOAST	154

Night 3: Touch

23.	A WALK ON THE WILD SIDE	167
24.	LOVE AT NIGHT	177
25.	SKIN-DEEP	188
26.	CRAZY BY NIGHT	195

Contents

Night 4: Scent

27. UNDERWORLD   209
28. SCENT OF A CITY   220
29. THE NOSE THAT KNOWS   226
30. GARDENS OF THE NIGHT   240

Night 5: Sight

31. THE BLACK-AND-WHITE MAN   255
32. FRENZY AND DARKNESS   266
33. BOUND FOR GLORY   279
34. WAITING   285
35. EXQUISITE CORPSE   297
36. MAGNETIC FIELDS   303
37. THE HOTEL OF GREAT MEN   308
38. THE HOUR OF CRIMES   314

Acknowledgments   323
Index   327

For Marie-Dominique and Louise—
Il n'y a qu'un bonheur dans la vie,
c'est d'aimer et d'être aimé.

And the night shall be filled with music,

And the cares that infest the day

Will fold their tents, like the Arabs,

And as silently steal away.

HENRY WADSWORTH LONGFELLOW, *The Day Is Done*

FIVE NIGHTS
IN
Paris

The Dangerous Edge

His words were shapely, even as his lips,
And courtesy he used like any lord.
"Was it through books that you first thought of ships?"
"Reading a book, sir, made me go abroad."

WILFRED OWEN, *It Was a Navy Boy*

Long before I decided to leave Australia, in the 1960s, I felt the desire to escape. Year by year, it crept over me like a thrilling sickness.

Some footloose friends also wanted to go abroad, but their horizons extended only to such tropical paradises as Bali. I set my sights on England and, in time, California.

Three factors forced the final break. Two were TV commercials. International airlines had just identified Australia as a rich new market and were upping their promotional efforts.

The first, for Pan Am, began with a telephoto lens peering down a runway. At the far end was a Boeing, lumbering toward us as it built up speed for the takeoff.

"At this moment," murmured an insinuatingly seductive voice, "in New York, the lights are going on along Broadway. Meanwhile, in London . . . ," and so on, through capsule evocations of Tokyo, Buenos Aires, Paris.

By then, the Boeing was swelling to fill the screen. "In this world," concluded the voice, "there are many places to go; many cities to see." And just as the plane roared overhead, came the clincher. "Now is the time," it said. "Now, when the heart says 'Go!' "

The second commercial, created by BOAC, later British Airways, was, by contrast, seductively soft-sell. For commentary, it offered simply a reading of John of Gaunt's anthem for England from Shakespeare's *Richard II.*

This royal throne of kings, this sceptered isle,
This earth of majesty, this seat of Mars

No roaring jet liners for the Brits; just scenes of villages, cities, lakes, woods, and fields, ending—a brilliant touch—with a man on a bicycle wobbling away down a leafy lane to "this earth, this realm, this *England*."

But I said there were three inspirations—and the third, perhaps the clincher, was nothing like the other two.

My wife of the time had a girlfriend from school. She'd recently married, so we invited the couple around for dinner. As my wife explained before they arrived, Annie had always been the wild one: the first to smoke, the first to play hooky, the first to lose her virginity.

In person, she certainly filled the eye: a little too much cleavage, perfume a bit overpowering, more hair than one was used to seeing in conservative Sydney. But undeniably a dish.

Her husband, Rob, was quieter. Big, casual, confident, soft-spoken; *Robert Mitchum*, I thought. He never quite said what he did for a living, but obviously it paid well. And he'd traveled to all the places I wanted to see.

Over dinner, I quizzed him mercilessly. What was New York really like? Had he been to Tokyo? London must be wonderful. And Paris?

"I've spent time there," he acknowledged.

I pressed for details. Where did he stay? What places did he visit? Notre Dame? The Louvre?

"For instance," I concluded, "last time you were in Paris, what was the first thing you did?"

He and Annie exchanged a look of collusion, one of those "Shall we tell them?" glances, with a half-grin, that often precede revelations.

"Well," said Rob, "if you really want to know, I knocked off the Patek Philippe watch exhibition."

I blinked. "Knocked off . . . ?"

"John, mate," he grinned, "I'm a *thief*."

And he was. A very good one, as it happens—the leader of a crew of shoplifters that targeted high-end stores all over the world. For the next few hours, he explained and demonstrated some tricks of his trade: the techniques of distraction and misdirection, the elements of performance, the *art* of it. The well-brought-up, law-abiding Catholic boy in me deprecated his way of life, but the larger part—the adventurer-in-waiting, the reader of crime fiction, the admirer of *film noir*—was seduced. After that, it was only a matter of time.

1

As Through a Glass, and Darkly

"I dare say, moreover," she pursued with an interested gravity, "that I do, that we all do here, run too much to mere eye. But how can it be helped? We're all looking at each other—and in the light of Paris one sees what things resemble. That's what the light of Paris seems always to show. It's the fault of the light of Paris—dear old light!"

HENRY JAMES, *The Ambassadors*

Some years ago, as a change from spending all my time writing, I began taking people on literary walks. It started by chance, when someone hired to lead such a walk for the Paris Writers' Workshop, of which I was codirector, didn't seem up to the task. To my surprise, I found I enjoyed it. However, a certain chill on the part of fellow writers made it clear they didn't approve. Apparently it Simply Wasn't Done. This just made me more determined.

Not only did it turn out to be great fun, and an opportunity to meet interesting people. It was also educational. I thought I knew my adoptive city pretty well. As it turned out, I was woefully ignorant.

My greatest problem proved to be where to take my clients. It wasn't that there was too little to show— rather, there was too much.

Asked how many expatriates worked in the arts in Montparnasse during the 1920s, writer and editor Robert McAlmon estimated 250. Not so many, perhaps— except that most lived within a mile of our apartment. Keeping track of these people and giving each of them a voice can be like trying to follow a single conversation in the din of a noisy party.

The period we call *les années folles*—the crazy years—is a blur of cocktails, jazz, and talk. Most memoirs of the period were written thirty years after the event, and often set out to settle old scores rather than provide an accurate record. Documentation is skimpy. Tape recorders weren't invented, and the only people taking notes were journalists, who felt free to improvise and invent. Facts and dates were of little account to them. Was Cole Porter actually in Paris in 1928 when he wrote the musical *Paris*? And did F. Scott Fitzgerald publish *The Great Gatsby* before or after he met Ernest Hemingway? With a deadline looming and too little time for research, it was easier to invent.

If chronicling the famous is difficult, how much more so those who never fulfilled their promise? Who today remembers Harold Stearns, George Davis, Hilda Doolittle, Glenway Wescott, Kay Boyle, Walter Berry, Mina Loy, Morley Callaghan, Elliot Paul, Harry Crosby? Yet all have voices just as loud as Hemingway or Stein. Once you add the other communities, such as the Spanish (Picasso painted *Guernica* a few blocks from our apartment), German (Wagner lived almost as close), Russian (Lenin drank at the Le Dôme café, on the other side of the Luxembourg Gardens), even the Australians (an Aussie painter named Agnes Goodsir actually lived in our apartment from 1919 to 1939), the conversations rise to a cacophony.

When Hemingway called Paris "a moveable feast," he didn't mention that there's no menu. The table sags under the weight of incidents, personalities, anecdotes, legends, lies. A century of remarkable achievement and extraordinary people has left traces everywhere. Tom Paine wrote *The Rights of Man* two doors away from our home. Contact Editions, which published Hemingway's first book, *Three Stories and Ten Poems*, was a little farther down the street. So was the city's most famous English-language bookshop Shakespeare & Company. Its proprietor, Sylvia Beach, publisher of *Ulysses*, had an apartment in our building . . . and that's just one street.

Paris is the ultimate museum. Other capitals demolish, renovate, and repurpose their great buildings and sell off their treasures, often looting those of other nations to replace them. By contrast, the French conserve, restore, and repair their architecture and cling to the work of their creative people. No country invests so much in protecting and sustaining its artists, whether writers, painters, filmmakers, or musicians. Each café, boutique, apartment building, or bookshop has not one story but several . . .

For anyone leading literary tours, it's a nightmare.

2

Woody's Nights

The best of America drifts to Paris. The American in Paris is the best American. It is more fun for an intelligent person to live in an intelligent country. France has the only two things toward which we drift as we grow older—intelligence and good manners.

F. SCOTT FITZGERALD

The first person to ask me "Do you do night walks?" was a staid middle-aged lady from Montreal.

Paris has no shortage of tours after dark, but few have literature on their mind. Most feature can-can girls at the Moulin Rouge and a visit to Pigalle's Museum of Eroticism. Somehow, she didn't seem the type.

Seeing my confusion, she went on: "I mean the same walks you do by day, but at night. There's this movie . . ."

Which is how I first heard of *Midnight in Paris*.

In Woody Allen's film, Gil Pender, a young American screenwriter and novelist visiting France with his fiancée, falls out of love with her and in love with Paris. During strolls alone at night, he's inexplicably transported back to the 1920s. There he meets Ernest Hemingway, Gertrude Stein, Scott and Zelda Fitzgerald, Djuna Barnes, even Salvador Dalí and his film director friend Luis Buñuel—to whom, in one of the film's best jokes, he outlines the plot of what would become Buñuel's milestone movie *The Exterminating Angel*. To Buñuel, however, the story of how guests at a dinner party, afflicted by inexplicable terror, refuse to leave, but settle down to squat in their hosts' home, in increasing squalor, makes no sense at all.

Midnight in Paris dodges the logistical difficulties of night walks. Gil doesn't stumble about too long on poorly lit streets before an antique Peugeot 176 picks him up and whisks him back to the *années folles*. After that, most of the action takes place indoors.

Sensibly, Allen also opts for entertainment over authenticity. He limits himself to the few years between the Great War and the crash of 1929 and concentrates on a dozen big names—most of whom, as it happens, were strangers to one another. If Cole Porter and Scott Fitzgerald ever met, for instance, history is silent on the

subject. Nor did French intellectuals such as Jean Cocteau party with the expats quite as intimately as Allen suggests, mostly because—one detail on which he's absolutely accurate—hardly any American expatriate spoke more than a few words of French.

A night walk around Paris would have to include some of the locations Woody used in his film, starting with the church of Saint-Étienne-du-Mont. Gil Pender is sitting on its steps when the vintage Peugeot carries him back to the 1920s. Nor should one forget the Crémerie Polidor on rue Monsieur-le-Prince. He goes there to meet Ernest Hemingway but, doubling back with an afterthought, finds it's become a laundromat. Usually scornful of Americans, the Polidor found Woody charming when he filmed there, even asking for a signed photograph to place in the window.

With *Midnight in Paris*, Allen embraced Paris almost as passionately as had Hemingway or Stein. This is ironic since, whatever he says these days, he didn't always love France. On the contrary, he was outspoken in his hostility.

He paid his first visit in 1964 to write and act in *What's New Pussycat* with Peter O'Toole and Peter Sellers, and loathed almost everything about it, in particular the food: both the ingredients and the way it was prepared. Despite living at the luxurious Hôtel George V, just off the Champs-Élysées, he shunned its restaurant and ate in a small café where, for eight months, he ordered the same meal every night: soup, sole meunière, and crème caramel. As he disliked being watched as he ate, and covered his mouth with his hand while he did so, he preferred to dine alone.

Mostly he kept to the hotel. Some nights he played poker, very profitably, or practiced the clarinet. The producer even found a rare example of the antique Rampone instrument he favored. Its hard, unyielding reed made it difficult to play, but the thin tone approximated that of the New Orleans jazz with which the adolescent Woody fell in love: jazz played on inferior instruments by men stiff in their fingers and short of breath—a shadow of Louis Armstrong's fiery music, and, for that reason, perversely satisfying to Allen. Years later, when he had become France's favorite foreigner, the Rampone factory dug out the blueprints and manufactured two new examples as a gift.

Woody did respect France's reverence for jazz and support for such American musicians as soprano saxophonist Sidney Bechet and pianist Bud Powell. Bechet came to Paris in the band accompanying Josephine Baker and made the city his home. But Bechet died in

1959, and in 1964 Powell had just returned to New York. Allen contented himself with getting to know, albeit tentatively, Claude Luter, France's senior virtuoso on the instrument. But as theme music for *Midnight in Paris* he would choose Bechet playing one of his own compositions, "Si Tu Vois Ma Mère."

The rest of the time, he worked on a play called *Don't Drink the Water*, which summarized everything he disliked about Europe. The main character, Walter Hollander, is a caterer from Newark. Trapped with his family by a revolution in the fictitious communist country of Vulgaria, he takes refuge in the American embassy, where he's at the mercy of a chef who uses ingredients that nauseate Hollander (and Woody)—oysters, hare, eel. Allen vented this dislike again in *Stardust Memories*, berating his housekeeper for trying to serve him rabbit. "I don't eat rodent!"

Given what happened on *What's New Pussycat*, his view of France was hardly surprising. They'd planned to shoot in Rome, but O'Toole, with memories of its paparazzi, persuaded the producer to relocate in Paris. Peter Sellers, who'd just recovered from a heart attack, was particularly obnoxious; he was determined to turn the film into a rerun of his success, *The Pink Panther*. Newly slimmed down, Sellers resembled Allen, and Woody wearied of being mistaken for him.

*Woody Allen (left), obviously less than enchanted with costars
Peter O'Toole and Peter Sellers in* What's New Pussycat.
(Larry Shaw/United Artists)

However it wasn't the food or Sellers that soured
Woody on Paris so much as a sexual disappointment so
humiliating that, in the words of Rhys Ifans in the film
Notting Hill, it would "make your balls shrink to the size
of raisins."

Among the crew of *Pussycat*, Woody was surprised
to see a face from his days as a coffeehouse comedian.
Vicky Tiel had worked at a Greenwich Village club, The

Duplex, where, in the scantily clad character of "Peaches LaTour," she introduced the acts and passed the hat afterward. As he was paid only what Tiel could coax out of the audience, Woody was grateful for her good looks and personality. Since then, she'd become a costume designer and was working with Mia Fonssagrives on some dresses for Paula Prentiss, cast in *Pussycat* as a Crazy Horse stripper named Liz Bien.

Tiel and Woody had a few dates in Paris, but she was already being pursued by the film's director, Clive Donner. The crew saw a way to settle the rivalry and celebrate Tiel's birthday at the same time. As Tiel explained later, "The crew told us, 'Look, this is the movie business! Everyone sleeps with everyone else, so you had better start joining in.' That's when they devised the competition between Clive and Woody, neither of whom had gotten as far as first base." She agreed to sleep with whichever of them produced the most lavish birthday gift. Donner offered the largest box of chocolates made by prestigious chocolatier Godiva, but Allen won with an American-style pinball machine.

Woody coached Tiel in the choreography of their big night. There would be no dinner, no small talk or foreplay of the sort that, in his films, so often goes wrong.

Instead, she was to come to his room, go straight to the bathroom, undress, and join him in bed. That night he waited, but she never came. At lunch that day, she met the man she later married—Ron Berkeley, makeup man for Richard Burton, who had a cameo in the film. "I fell in love with Ron on the spot," says Tiel, "and went to bed with him straight away. It was only in the morning I realized I'd been supposed to spend the night with Woody. The next time I saw him was the following morning on the set. He was absolutely devastated. He'd spent the evening getting himself ready and planning what we were going to do." Woody found consolation in a classically Allenesque manner. His girlfriend Louise Lasser rang from New York with the news that her mother had committed suicide. He invited her to join him in Paris. She remained there for the rest of the shoot, and they married in 1966.

It took almost forty years, but Allen forgave Paris. It helped that the French embraced him and his films with an admiration denied him by the United States. In *Everyone Says I Love You*, he played a grudging expatriate who overcomes his loathing for snails in order to seduce Julia Roberts, but with *Midnight in Paris* he fell into the city's arms. Paris had waited for him.

3

Under Cover

ROMAN JOURNALIST: *"What was the happiest day of your life?"*
MOVIE STAR ANITA EKBERG: *"It was a night, darling."*
  La Dolce Vita

Even as a boy, I was only at home in the shade.

On picnics, while everyone else raced down the beach and into the surf, I retreated, book in hand, to the shelter of a tree. Other families, hauling coolers filled with beer and sodas, observed me narrowly as they passed. "Poor kid," they thought. What ailed me, to be deprived of our nation's greatest blessing? If they had known I avoided it by choice, they'd have thought me out of my mind. An Australian not enjoying sun? Imagine a polar bear in Maui and you'll grasp the improbability.

The more I resisted, the harder my parents pushed.

"Why aren't you outside, dear?" my mother asked. Parting the curtains on our front window, she squinted into blue-white sunlight so fierce that, had the solar panel been invented, a few could have powered the entire town. "Always with your nose stuck in a book," she continued. "You should be playing sport."

As most sports required me to stand in the sun while someone more motivated flung a ball at my head, the suggestion drove me even deeper into the shadows. Raising my book higher, I returned to whatever alternative universe was sheltering me that week. Soon I was lost again in the deep space of *Astounding Science Fiction Magazine*, the Vienna of Graham Greene's *The Third Man*, or Raymond Chandler's Los Angeles, where "the streets were dark with something more than night." I was home.

To be fair, some of my dissatisfaction was genetic. Our family had a tradition of not quite obeying the rules. During World War II, my father, a pastry cook and baker, owned a shop in King's Cross, Sydney's tenderloin, the equivalent of New York's Greenwich Village, London's Soho, Berlin's Reeperbahn. Once the U.S. Navy made our city its base, sailors crowded the streets, looking for a girl, a drink, and a snack—

roughly in that order. But while birds and booze were on offer in quantity, they searched in vain for a hot dog or hamburger and positively recoiled from local baked goods: lumpy cookies riddled with raisins, mystery-meat pies, and British-style buns, sticky with frosting.

Dad took action. As each USN ship docked, he could be found loitering outside the Woolloomooloo navy yard with a cabdriver friend. Buttonholing enlisted men wearing the crescent *C* on their left sleeve that signified a baker or cook, they offered a free ride to the depravities of "The Cross"—preceded by a few glasses of powerful local beer to toast Australian-American relations. Quite soon, the cook, in one of my mother's aprons, would be at work in our kitchen, demonstrating his recipe for brownies, while my father watched over his shoulder and took notes.

Too young to have seen all this at first hand, I had to rely on anecdotes and a few bits of evidence kicking around the house. One was a shoebox filled with Bakelite plaques from the wartime shop window where they had identified the American-style items on offer: angel food cake, applesauce cake, chocolate chip cookies. Who knew how they tasted—except that they must be heaven?

More permanent keepsakes of those times included

a Zippo cigarette lighter, a tarnished silver money clip, and, my favorite, a pair of aviator-style mirror sunglasses. Their steel rims, springy metal earpieces, and large green lenses made me look, I thought, quite dashing, even a little like the masked hero in my favorite American comic book, *The Spirit*. As I cycled around town wearing them, neighbors stared, particularly after I rode my bike into a couple of lampposts. Following the third such accident, I retired the glasses, since I thought I'd made my point.

In quieter moments, I wondered what exactly was wrong with disliking sun. Sailors didn't spend their holidays on ocean cruises, and while Arabs tolerated sand, they'd take a shady oasis any day. As King Feisal explains to T. E. Lawrence in the film *Lawrence of Arabia*, "No Arab loves the desert. We love water and green trees. There is nothing in the desert—and no man needs nothing." But Lawrence, dismissed by Feisal as "another of those desert-loving English," isn't convinced. Asked to suggest something in favor of the desert, he says, "It's clean." In his petulant tone, I recognized the righteousness of the parents and teachers who lectured me on the joys of sun.

So when I came to Europe, it was in flight from their belief. I saw myself strolling under Tuscan grape arbors,

gondola-gliding down Venetian canals, or punting between Cambridge's ancient stone walls, dripping and
cool. In time, I would experience all of these, and more,
until I had almost drunk my fill of shade.

But it wasn't until I moved to France that I got to
know the night.

4

The Dark Side

Never was anything great achieved without danger.
NICCOLO MACHIAVELLI

Mae West, the most voluptuous and outrageous actress of Hollywood in the 1930s, said of temptation, "Given the choice between two evils, I always go for the one I never tried before." To choose neither never entered her mind, or mine. In fact, the more I was urged to Do The Right Thing, the less inclined I was to obey.

This has made me the most intransigent kind of tourist. Though I lived in London for fourteen years, I never visited the Tower of London or watched the Changing of the Guard. When I lived in Dublin, those fans of James Joyce's *Ulysses* who spend each June 16 following the path of Leopold Bloom around the city had to do so without me. And though I've been to the Louvre numerous times since I moved to Paris, I have never, in more than twenty years, been within touching distance of the Venus de Milo or the Mona Lisa.

On my first visit to New York, I did take a bus tour as far as the Cathedral of Saint John the Divine, but I stopped to try my hand at what, in those days, was the exotic diversion of playing Frisbee and was left behind. Deciding to walk back to my hotel, I found myself attending a block party, eating my first chicken-fried steak, and finally drinking bourbon in a bar with someone whom, I realized later, was almost certainly . . . well, that incident belongs in some other book.

I'm also that nightmare of the tour guide, the know-it-all. Being led round San Simeon, William Randolph Hearst's mansion on the hills above the California coast, I challenged the claim of the Parks Service guide that Hearst had been a pious model citizen and his relationship with live-in girlfriend Marion Davies that of an affectionate uncle to his wayward niece.

Pointing to the figure of the virgin over the entrance to a chapel, I asked, "Then how do you explain what Dorothy Parker wrote about that?"

"Go on," the guide said tersely.

"There are various versions," I said, "but one goes something like:

I swear on my honor
I saw a madonna
Standing in a niche
Above the door
Of a prominent whore
Of a prominent son of a bitch."

This amused the other visitors. Even the guide unbent a little. But he hung back as we walked to the next point of interest and murmured, "I heard it as 'the world's worst son of a bitch.' But do me a favor, would you, and keep this stuff to yourself? I've gotta earn a living here."

I have a long history of walking through those half-open doors or gates that warn NO ADMITTANCE or ENTER AT YOUR OWN RISK. In Dublin, a scholar of recent history helped me track down the haunts of those who died in the rising of Easter 1916, the rebellion of which W.B. Yeats wrote "a terrible beauty is born." In London, a dealer in antique silver took me at four in the morning to the clandestine thieves' market known as The Stones, where anything sold before the sun comes up remains, no matter how suspicious its provenance, the property of the buyer.

Some encounters were more comic than mysterious, or, occasionally, both. In Los Angeles, I attended the running of the grunion on a beach near Malibu. While people scrambled and squealed with flashlights at the water's edge, scooping the twitching fish into plastic buckets, I admired the lovely Sandra Tsing Loh, seated at a white grand piano, as she led a chamber orchestra in her composition "Night of the Grunion."

Most of these events took place at night, often in the early hours. And the writers I most admire are those who write about such times with a special intensity. A few like to quote Robert Browning:

> *Our interest's on the dangerous edge of things.*
> *The honest thief, the tender murderer,*
> *The superstitious atheist.*

By "dangerous," they didn't mean physical adventure; none of these men climbed mountains nor went white-water rafting. They meant the unconventional— that sense of turning a corner or opening a door without quite knowing what to expect.

Paris has innumerable such corners and doors. I seek them out, as I sought their equivalent in other cities. Some are best seen by day. Others, like certain night-blooming flowers, reveal their perfume after sunset. But they have this in common: to gain admittance, one merely has to reach out and push that gate that stands slightly ajar . . .

Promenades

I don't care what you've ever done
With don't care who
But walkin' is my favorite thing
For cats and chicks to do.
    DAVE LAMBERT, *"Walkin' "*

Parisians love to walk. For reasons, you need to go back quite a long way.

Before the invention of movable type and mass printing, a Greek or Latin text often existed in a single copy held in a remote monastery. Forget interlibrary loans. The monks guarded their volumes jealously, sometimes even chaining them to the shelves of the scriptorium. To study the texts, a scholar might have to walk halfway across France. During the Middle Ages, a significant proportion of travelers on the roads of France were the monks known as peripatetics, or walkers. They belonged

Saint Denis loses his head

to many different religious orders. What united them was a willingness to hit the road in search of wisdom.

Saint Denis, Paris's patron saint, set the tone. After the local Roman governor decapitated him in the third century for daring to speak his mind, Denis is said to have picked up his severed head and walked six miles, declaiming a sermon every foot of the way—another

Paris habit that flourishes still. For a Parisian, walking with someone and not talking at the same time is like eating a hot dog without mustard.

The urge to take long journeys is etched deep in Gallic DNA. Before the revolution of 1789, the kings of France, though based in Versailles or the Louvre, spent part of the year traveling to the regions, usually with a retinue of a few hundred courtiers. This made good sense. It not only reminded the local aristocracy who was boss. The royal train could also freeload on them and get in some decent hunting in forests that hadn't been denuded of game.

In July and August, the urban French still drop everything and return to the region of their ancestors. Whether a château in the Dordogne or a campsite outside Marseilles, every French man and woman regards some piece of soil as crucially important to his or her existence. At the same time, over a hundred thousand people, many from France, make the pilgrimage, mostly on foot, to the shrine of Saint James in the Cathedral of Santiago de Compostela in northwestern Spain. The tendency to travel long distances on foot is one the French respect even in foreigners. In the autumn of 1878, Robert Louis Stevenson toured mountainous south-central France. His *Travels with a Donkey in the*

A musicians café, 1930s

Cévennes won many friends in France because, explained a local historian, "he showed us the landscape that makes us who we are." (Stevenson paid no such compliment to his own people, the Scots, summing up his suspicion of them in his most famous story, *Dr. Jekyll and Mr. Hyde*.)

From the moment Baron Haussmann rebuilt Paris in the 1860s as a city of wide sidewalks, the locals decided that certain avenues and squares were exceptionally pleasant just as places to hang out. Often the reasons were practical; the French are nothing if not rational. Streets near universities attracted scholars, journalists, and bookworms. In others, artists' models, band musicians, chorus singers, and bit players in theater or cabaret gathered, making it easy for potential employers to find them. At cafés opposite theaters, such as the Procope, across the road from the Comédie Française, and Café Voltaire, facing the Théâtre de l'Odéon, writers and critics met, while the streets around the market quarter of Les Halles filled with accommodating young women and *hôtels de passe* that rented rooms by the hour.

During the 1920s, a person's preferred café was also his contact address. The Dôme, the Rotonde, and the Ritz Bar had racks for mail. As Jacqueline Goddard, one of Man Ray's models, explained to me:

> *After a day of work, the artists wanted to get away from their studios and get away from what they were creating. They all met in the cafés to argue about this and that, to discuss their work, politics, and philosophy. We went to the bar of La Coupole. Bob, the barman, was a terribly nice chap. As there was no telephone in those days, everybody used him to leave messages. At the Dôme, we also had a little*

*place behind the door for messages. The telephone
was the death of Montparnasse.*

Certain squares and alleys attracted sellers of food.
As most rented rooms had no kitchens, people bought
their food already prepared: coffee, hot milk, bread and
rolls in the morning; cheese, sausage, boiled potatoes,
soup, or stew later in the day.

But modern Paris had no place for street sellers.
Haussmann's new Paris, accessible to pedestrians, encouraged vendors to move indoors, creating shops
which were restocked each day from the markets at Les
Halles. Even bread, the staple for most people, was only
sold on its day of baking. In one of its first reforms, the
Commune, the anarchist government that briefly ruled
Paris in 1871, freed bakers from having to work through
the night to guarantee warm baguettes in the morning.

To see the cheap food of the nineteenth-century
poor, you need to visit rural markets. Butchers still sell
pale horse meat steaks devoid of fat, or tripe, or whole
beef tongues, sometimes still steaming from the *mar-
mite* where they've just been boiled. In a form of reverse
snobbery, some of Paris's better butchers and fishmon-
gers have revived the old methods. They "draw" a
chicken in front of you, inquiring if you wish to keep

the liver and other edible organs—a few even maintain a gas flame to singe pin feathers—while a good *poissonnier* will still gut and fillet your fish, a service for which, traditionally, one leaves a small tip.

Refrigeration and better hygiene forced street vendors indoors, but the habit persisted of trading only with trusted local sellers. Whom they patronized became a matter of keen competition among cooks, and remains so. Each swears by the cheese from a certain *fromager* or insists on a particular *chocolatier*, and dinner parties can expire in tight-lipped confrontations over the best place to buy rhubarb. With supermarkets on almost every block, Parisians still stubbornly insist on *their* choice— hence the Paris institution known as *la griffe*.

La griffe is the pattern of one's walk around the city on a shopping day. Strictly speaking, it means "claw," or the mark made by talons scratching a tree, but in practice it's one's signature, the mark that signifies ownership of a territory.

Mine is well established. I seldom buy meat except from the butcher in the food hall of the Marché Saint-Germain. A vendor just across the aisle from him remains my first port of call for fruit and vegetables. Logically, on leaving the market, I should get my bread at Mulot, one of the best local *boulangers* and *pâtissiers*—

except that I like the *pain au fromage* baked by Kayser on rue de l'Ancienne Comédie, and so I make a three-block detour to buy a loaf warm from the oven. The Kayser baker scatters grated Gruyère on top, which leaves a crust of melted cheese around the edges, delicious for nibbling as I follow the invisible path of my *griffe* into rue de Buci and a coffee at my favorite café, Au Chai de l'Abbaye.

And it was my *griffe* that led me to the solution of my problem about night walks.

Five Ladies Feeling

All credibility, all good conscience, all evidence of truth come only from the senses.
FRIEDRICH NIETZSCHE

Tour companies offering Paris holidays often proposed "five nights" in the city, but they really meant five days. Attractions dwindle at night. Except for the Louvre, which stays open to 8.45 p.m. on Wednesdays and Fridays, most museums, parks, and galleries close when the sun goes down. Was there really no more stimulating way to spend an evening in Paris than an American movie, a four-course dinner on a *bateau-mouche*, or a stroll down the Champs-Élysées?

But the effectiveness of a guided tour depended on being able to point things out. How could that be done in darkness?

In his novel *Cadillac Jack*, detailing the adventures of an antique hunter, Larry McMurtry elucidates the key concept of collecting—everything has to be somewhere. As with finding Tiffany lamps or Revere silver, solving any problem is largely a question of waiting until the information reveals itself. Somewhere, in some corner of the city, Paris had the answer to my problem. I just had to let it in.

As it wasn't part of my *griffe*, I didn't often pass the Musée National du Moyen Age, the museum of the Middle Ages housed in the old abbey of Cluny on the corner of boulevard Saint-Germain and boulevard Saint-Michel. The Cluny demands more attention than I give it, but its lamenting saints and agonized Christs always leave me feeling morose. One can't just slip in for a few moments as I often do with the Église Saint-Sulpice or the former chapel of Maria de' Medici's palace, these days the Musée de Luxembourg. Rather, the Cluny's a place for wet Wednesdays in February, the architectural equivalent of those scratchy goat-hair shirts once worn by penitent monks. I wouldn't have visited it on this occasion if they had not been digging up the sidewalk on boulevard Saint-Michel. Crossing to avoid the roadworks brought me up against the railings around it, and something clicked.

The doorman peered into my carrier, grimaced at the bunch of celery sticking out the top, but placed it behind his desk without asking why someone would choose, in the middle of the morning's shopping, to browse a museum of medieval antiquity.

My visit was brief. I needed to look at only one room—the one displaying the tapestries of the Lady and the Unicorn.

These six hangings cover the walls of a circular room at the heart of the museum, kept in gloom to preserve their colors. This morning, the gallery was almost empty, so, rather than peering over the heads of coach parties from Yokohama or Capetown, I could approach them almost close enough to touch.

Woven around the time of Columbus, they ended up in the Château de Boussac in central France. Who made them and why are mysteries still unsolved. Supposedly a Prince Zizim, pretender to the Ottoman Empire and a prisoner in the château, commissioned them for his fiancée back in Constantinople. In the 1480s, Pierre d'Aubusson did capture Cem Sultan, half brother of Sultan Bayezid II, who paid well to keep him there. However there's no record that Cem ever visited Boussac or ordered any tapestries.

They were rediscovered in the nineteenth century

by novelist Georges Sand. She alerted fellow writer and amateur archaeologist Prosper Mérimée. Best known for writing the story on which Bizet based the opera *Carmen*, Mérimée, in one of those appointments one can't imagine being made anywhere but France, was also inspector-general of ancient monuments. Horrified that visitors were snipping pieces as souvenirs, he campaigned to acquire them for the nation.

All six show a similar scene. On a deep red background strewn with blossoms, a woman in a robe, accompanied by her maid, dallies with a lion and a unicorn while rabbits, ferrets, and squirrels scamper among the grass and wildflowers. In the first of the series, the maid pumps the bellows of a portative organ as her mistress picks out a tune. In another, she offers her a box of candies, and in a third the lady toys with a wreath of flowers, one of which her pet monkey sniffs. The sixth tapestry incorporates the enigmatic text "*À mon seul désir,*" which might mean "To my sole desire" or "by my will alone," or, at a stretch, "love desires only beauty of soul."

When I emerged after just ten minutes, the guard rolled his eyes and handed back my groceries, assuming I'd just dropped in to use the toilet. In fact, I'd wanted to confirm something I'd read years before—that the tapestries were inspired by the five senses. The organ represents hearing, the candy relates to taste, the monkey's flower signifies smell, and so on.

Why not base my night walks on the five senses? If they were sufficient for the master of the Lady and the Unicorn, they should be good enough for me.

The Lady and the Unicorn

7

The Right Way to Write

Black as the devil, hot as hell, pure as an angel,
sweet as love.

CHARLES MAURICE DE TALLEYRAND on his
preferences in coffee

S ome fallacies about Paris have put down roots like cultural crab grass, never to be totally eradicated. Generally they can be traced to a novel, a screenplay, a song, or, occasionally, an American veteran recalling, not very accurately, a few gaudy days on leave in 1918.

One myth that clings like a burr is the vision of writers scribbling in Paris cafés. Harry Potter author J. K. Rowling gave added credence to this when she said that "the idea of wandering off to a café with a notebook and writing and seeing where that takes me for a while is just bliss." Not everyone agrees. Canadian novelist and long-time Paris resident Mavis Gallant wrote:

The other day I was asked, in all seriousness,
where one can see authors at work in cafés. It
sounded for all the world like watching chimpanzees
riding tricycles: both are unnatural occupations.
I have only one friend who still writes her novels
in notebooks, in cafés. She chooses cafés that are
ordinary and charmless, favoring one for a time,
then another, as one does with restaurants. Some are
near home; many involve a long bus trip. If anyone
she knows discovers the café, she changes at once for
another, more obscure, hard to get to.

Anyone sucking a pen in a Paris café today is probably a freshman from the Oatmeal, Nebraska, Community College, wondering what to write on a postcard after "Having wonderful time. Wish you were here." Professional writers seldom put pen to paper in public, and that goes double for the French. One is as likely to find an author practicing his trade in a café as, say, a dentist.

Of course, he may have an ulterior motive. Edmund White, American novelist and biographer of Jean Genet, was, with his dog Fred, a regular at the chic Café Beaubourg, next to the Centre Pompidou. On the way back to his apartment on the Île Saint-Louis, he always paused by the grille supplying air to l'Institut de Recherche et Coordination Acoustique/Musique, aka IRCAM, the avant-garde musical workshop under the building. He did this so Fred could defecate into the grating—payback to Pierre Boulez, head of IRCAM, who had refused White an interview.

Hemingway was one of the last authors to write in a café—specifically the Closerie des Lilas. He called it "the nearest good café when we lived in the flat over the sawmill at 113 rue Notre-Dame-des-Champs, and it was one of the best cafés in Paris. It was warm inside in the winter and in the spring and fall it was fine outside with the table under the shade of the trees on the side where the statue of Marshal Ney was, and the square, regular tables under the big awnings along the boulevard." Most expats preferred those cafés clustered around the intersection of boulevard de Montparnasse and boulevard Raspail. The Closerie, many blocks away, at the top of the Luxembourg Gardens, conformed to the rule of Mavis Gallant's friend by being well away from distraction. It offered Hemingway what he most craved as he wrote—seclusion and quiet.

These days, the cafés where Hemingway and Sartre held court have been transformed. Today's moneymaker is food, not coffee and conversation. For a sense of Paris as it was in the *années folles* or in the hot postwar days of existentialism, Christian Dior's New Look, and the jazz clubs of Saint-Germain-des-Prés, you need to move away from the Flore, Deux Magots, Dôme, or Coupole. Tourism has transformed these one-time bohemian hangouts into "sites" where nostalgia is an item on the menu, and an expensive one at that.

But visitors in town for just the obligatory five days and nights seldom travel far from the central arrondissements. They never see Café Fleurus or the Rendezvous, or the Wepler on place de Clichy, preferred loitering place of Henry Miller, who anatomized its culture of semiresident prostitutes so precisely in *Quiet Days in Clichy*, or the Tournon, solitary and isolated next to the Luxembourg Gardens, and, perhaps because of its equidistance from both Montparnasse and Saint-Germain-des-Prés, favored by the postwar African American community—James Baldwin, Chester Himes, Richard Wright—and the next wave of postwar expatriates like Alexander Trocchi, Richard Seaver, and Christopher Logue, who paid their rent writing pseudonymous porn novels for Maurice Girodias's Olympia Press.

I'd often had coffee at the Tournon with Hazel Rowley, Richard Wright's Australian biographer. Wright's ghost, irascible and aggrieved, seemed to haunt the place, along with the spirits of other black Americans of those days, most of whom had a good reason to keep out of the bright lights and away from the suspicious eyes of boulevard Saint-Germain. Many had drug problems; some were communists; almost none were in France entirely legally. The Tournon also acted as a magnet to those women attracted to African Americans as sex partners. "All of us vocal blacks collected there to choose our white women for each night," wrote Himes in his memoirs, "and the white women gathered about us and waited our selection."

The Tournon drew other renegades as well. In her memoir of Paris in the 1950s, April Ashley, formerly George Jamieson of Liverpool and a pioneer of transgender surgery, described her expedition into that corner of *bohème*. Ordering a kir, she chatted up Wright, whose novel *Native Son* she'd read. Ashley thought he "looked sad, a long way from home."

"Then why don't you go back to Mississippi?" she asked.

"And wipe spit off my face all day?" snapped Wright.

Ashley's sense of exclusion made her a perceptive observer of existential Paris. To the intellectuals of Saint-Germain-des-Prés, her search for a new physical identity paralleled their own attempts at social and cultural redefinition. She was also a witness to the twilight of at least one god.

Hemingway materialized there occasionally, still the great literatus but increasingly lushed to bits and surrounded by nobodies and even, sometimes, Parisians. A tab accompanied each drink and in due course they would all find their way across to Hemingway's area of table. By the end of a stint, he'd often have fifty or sixty under his chin. Before his eyes finally glazed over, he would pay them all and stumble out. Someone might shout "La musique!" as a way of clearing the slightly perplexed air Hemingway always left behind him. We'd be off to the Club Tabou or to L'Ange Bleu, or the Club Saint-Germain where Stéphane Grappelli swung his violin, or uptown to Le Boeuf sur le Toit where Juliette Greco sang her chansons réalistes *as if she were hacking her way through a jungle.*

8

White Nights

It's not a pretty face, I grant you, but underneath its
flabby exterior is an enormous lack of character.

OSCAR LEVANT on himself as pianist Adam Cook
in the 1951 screenplay of *An American in Paris.*

Terrance Gelenter (left) with François, owner of the
restaurant Au Bon Saint Pourçain

Not much of importance takes place in Paris without discussion in the cafés, so I made the rounds

with the night walk idea. In particular, I consulted Terrance Gelenter.

If I were honest, I'd admit that Terrance has more right to be considered a true expatriate than myself. Having married into a French family, I'm what the locals call *métis*— part French. Terrance, however, remains unregenerately alien, an outsider and happy to be so.

Resourcefully, he's turned this ambiguity and love of Paris into a livelihood. He's Mr. Paris, the go-to guy for every tourist need, from a chauffeur to greet you off the plane at Roissy to . . . well, he's never defined the limits of his hospitality skills, but they're far-reaching.

It had been his idea, five years ago, that I should give literary walks—a suggestion in return for which, originally, he demanded 50 percent of my fee. We terminated this arrangement once people began to approach me directly—which he took as the green light to start leading tours himself. Since then, introducing visitors to *flanerie*—strolling—has become one of his many meal tickets.

Lately, he's branched out into singing. A bathroom baritone of modest attainments, he could be heard two nights a week in the lounge of a boutique hotel in the fourteenth arrondissement, mangling the repertoire of Cole Porter and Jerome Kern. His performances made

me think of a review that appeared in a British newspaper when Simone Signoret was rash enough to play
Lady Macbeth opposite Alec Guinness in 1966. At last,
said the critic, a means existed to identify who really
wrote the plays attributed to Shakespeare. One simply
had to post an observer near the grave of each candidate
and note which one turned over when Mme. Signoret
came onstage.

Terrance was easiest to find on Sunday mornings,
when he received his admirers at a table in Café Flore,
but I caught up with him midweek on his cell phone.

"Sure, *bubeleh*." Even after a decade in France, the
Brooklyn in his voice remained as pungent as a kosher
pickle. "In fact, let's have lunch."

I couldn't hide my surprise. "You're buying me
lunch?"

"Who said 'buy'? We go dutch."

He suggested La Petite Perigourdine, on rue des
Écoles, the street that runs through the Sorbonne university district. Cafés around universities are usually
cheap, and this one lived up to that tradition with a
modest prix fixe lunch.

Even at noon, most tables were full. By the door, a
rack of varnished pigeonholes held rolled napkins, a sur-
vival from the days when regulars used the same napkin

all week and stored it in a pigeonhole until it accumulated enough stains to be worth washing. This practice shocked some visitors to France during the *belle époque*. One was Lord Curzon, former viceroy of India. When an aide explained that not every diner could expect a fresh napkin with each meal, his lordship exclaimed, "Can there be such poverty?"

Terrance was already installed at a table by the wall, where a large window gave an unparalleled view of pedestrians toiling up and down the steep slope of rue des Carmes. As I watched, a short skirt and some pretty legs in high heels appeared on the right-hand side of the big window and moved down to the left. A few seconds later, a pair of hips in skin-tight jeans appeared on the left and, muscles tensing under the denim, progressed to the right.

I slipped into the banquette opposite him. No need to ask why this place appealed.

"I hear they serve food here as well," I said. He tore himself away from his private beauty parade.

"I'm studying the menu."

"So I see. The French have a word for you."

He waggled his eyebrows à la Groucho Marx. *"Adorable? Séduisant?"*

"Try again."

While the French vocabulary is smaller than that of English, it loads certain words with additional meaning.

The one I had in mind for Terrance was *roué*.

It means, literally, "wheeled," and recalls the medieval method of execution which tied the criminal to a wagon wheel in the public square while his bones were broken one by one with an iron bar. As such horrors died out, a *roué* came to mean a criminal who deserved such treatment, then, in time, any man who behaved badly, particularly with women: what they called in Edwardian England a "bounder" or a "cad." Even after the French widened their dictionary of seduction to include *tombeur* (a serial seducer who, Casanova-like, induces women to fall—*tomber*—for him), and *dragueur* (someone who dredges or trawls in search of sex), *roué* survived to define the man who indulges in all three, but unashamedly, and with a little style. It suited Terrance perfectly.

Just then the waiter arrived, and we switched subjects while we ordered, and waited for our *confit de canard aux pommes de terres à l'anglaise*. A couple of tables away, some Americans were struggling to order lunch. While they puzzled over the menu, the waiter stood by, order pad in hand, staring over their heads and all but tapping his foot in exasperation. The fact that patrons sit while waiters stand gives the latter an automatic superiority.

What if diners stood to order, or the waiter sat down at the table to take it? The idea was so revolutionary it would probably bring down the government.

"Night walks?" Terrance said as I explained my plan. "You mean like a *nuit blanche*?"

"Not exactly . . ."

From June 11 to July 2, around Saint Petersburg in northwestern Russia, the sun remains just below the horizon all night long, bathing the world's most northerly city in pearly luminescence. Locals call these *belye nochi*—white nights. Though similar conditions produce the same effect across Scandinavia, where it's called "the midnight sun," only in Saint Petersburg do such nights induce that introspection bordering on despair which inspired Dostoyevsky to write an entire book about it.

Nothing so drastic takes place during the continental summer, but the French, undeterred, fell in love with the concept, applying it to any night made sleepless by restlessness. *La nuit blanche* joined *le weekend*, *le strip-tease*, and *le hamburger* among foreign terms rebranded as French.

"I don't know," Gelenter mused. "Couldn't it be dangerous?"

"Oh, you mean what happened to Delanoë."

In 2001, Paris's then-mayor, Bertrand Delanoë,

designated either the first Saturday or the first Sunday of October as an official *nuit blanche*. Cafés and clubs were urged to stay open, and musicians and performers to give shows in the streets. He held open house at the Hôtel de Ville for anyone who cared to drop by. This became an annual event, even after an out-of-work computer technician turned up at the town hall in 2002 and, announcing he didn't like either homosexuals or politicians—Delanoë was both—stabbed him, fortunately without fatal result. After that, the mayor, while no less hospitable, traveled with a bodyguard.

Very few people ask me about the risks of Paris streets, and, to tell the truth, they're negligible. It is a brave thief who tries a holdup when every gendarme carries a pistol and all are trained in martial arts. Our apartment has been burgled, but *cambrioleurs* seldom steal books or paintings, and we are obviously not the kind of people who leave diamond bracelets lying about. The greatest risk is pickpocketing, which has reached almost industrial proportions on the métro, thanks to an influx of gifted operators from eastern Europe who prefer to collect aid from the prosperous west by direct means rather than going through the bureaucracy of Strasbourg.

But Gelenter wasn't talking about robbery.

"What about the streets? You don't want to walk about on those at night. The cobbles are murder."

He was right. Older streets offer gaps just waiting to trap a heel. And staircases were often uneven and poorly lit. In old age, the actress Arletty became almost blind. She recruited young actor François Périer to guide her on formal occasions. Notorious for her language, the star of *Les Enfants du Paradis* gave Périer a hard time. On one of their first outings, when he murmured, "Steps ahead," she snapped, "Steps up or steps down, asshole?"

Though Terrance and I continued discussing night walks over a couple of coffees and a sorbet, the moment "between the pear and the cheese," where, traditionally, the French deal with business, passed without a conclusion. There were simply too many wheres, hows, and for whoms to counterbalance the why nots.

My last memory as I left the café was of Terrance lingering over a second *express*, his attention riveted by the passing parade of rue des Carmes—a man at peace with the world.

9

Noises at Night

If I can't see Paris when I open my eyes in the morning,
I want to go right back to sleep.

HEDY LAMARR in *Algiers*

Though it alerted me to some potential drawbacks to night walks, Gelenter's skepticism didn't discourage me. True, there were problems, but some had already been solved.

The cobbles, for instance. Existing Paris-by-night tours ducked this difficulty by going indoors, to the cabarets and nightclubs of Pigalle. Though, inconveniently for me, most literary sites closed their doors just as these hot spots opened for business, there were sure to be some cultural locations sufficiently well lit to be accessible after dark.

And once I began thinking about the idea, material accumulated. For a scent walk, for instance: medieval monks planted rosemary and thyme between the stones of the paths around their medicinal herb gardens so that feet, crushing the plants, released their aroma. With a precedent like that, there must be places where the night brought out Paris's unique perfume.

As for taste, with eating approaching a religion in Paris, such a walk should be a pushover. In Italy and Spain, American colleges were already offering courses in culinary studies where "classes" took place at various restaurants and the only required reading was the menu. Surely one could do the same thing in Paris. A friend already conducted U.S. high school seniors on a food-and-drink course, somewhat hampered by the participants not being allowed alcohol. I'd given talks to her class and noted their slightly aggrieved expressions. In their position, I'd feel exactly the same way.

Nor would a touch walk pose problems in so tactile a city—although art historian Walter Benjamin lamented how a preoccupation with "sights" and stories prevents us from smelling or literally feeling a building or street. The true *flaneur*, he said, "would be happy to trade all his knowledge of artists' quarters, birthplaces and princely palaces for the scent of a single weathered threshold or the touch of a single tile—which any old dog carries away."

As for a sound walk, I hadn't given it much thought. Modern Paris wasn't a particularly audible city—not by comparison with the 1930s, when the streets of Saint-Germain-des-Prés and Montparnasse were a cacophony, particularly on Saturday nights. Nobody back then appeared to mind. If anything, it was part of Paris's charm. In 1935, humorist E. B. White favorably contrasted Paris street sounds with those of New York. To him, Manhattan noise "has an irritant quality, full of sharp distemper. It is impatient, masochistic—unlike the noise of Paris, where the shrill popping of high-pitched horns spreads gaiety and slightly drunken good humor." These bulb horns, honked aggressively, mostly by taxi drivers were as distinctive an aural signature of Paris in the 1920s as the piano accordion. Larry Hart wrote them into "That's the Song of Paree"—"We have taxi horns and klaxons / To scare the Anglo-Saxons"—while George Gershwin took a collection of taxi horns back to New York and scored a passage of *An American in Paris* for four of them.

Mavis Gallant wrote about a similar impulse.

A young composer, in Paris for the first time, told me how he heard Paris rather than saw it, how he envisioned Paris sound in all its shapes and forms. The shape of the sound of Paris traffic is different from the sound of New York and Toronto. He drew or shaped those sounds in air with his hands. Since

then, it was just a few weeks ago, I have been
listening to familiar street noise and trying to see
what he meant, but I attach words and images to
sounds. Cars moving along rue de Vaugirard are
like gushing water, turned on and off.

I tried this a few times, but after being almost run down by a bus on boulevard Saint-Michel, better sense prevailed.

Seeing images in sounds sounded like another version of what John Ruskin called the "pathetic fallacy"— the belief that states of mind can be reflected in nature. Bad fiction and worse poetry is filled with armies advancing as dark clouds build, lovers surrendering to passion in the gush and roar of a thunderstorm, or that old favorite of melodrama, the return of hope with the rising of the sun: as the silent movie title cards put it, "Came the Dawn." In short, the impossibility of finding cues for a sound walk was calling the whole idea into question—until, that is, I met Jesse Joe Callaway.

One moment, I was dawdling over a café crème at Au Chai de l'Abbaye. The next, a massive figure subsided into the seat opposite.

"Hey, hoss!" it growled. "How's ya hammer hangin'?" He offered a meaty paw. "Jesse Joe Callaway."

Early in my guiding career, I'd taken three large ladies from Amarillo, Texas, on a stroll through Montparnasse. At the start, it hadn't gone well. None of them were interested in literature, and I watched their enthusiasm fade by the minute. Fortunately, we paused outside the premises of master *chocolatier* Christian Constant on rue de Fleurus, around the corner from Gertrude Stein's old apartment. One sniff of his rich dark Grenache spiced with cayenne fired up their appetite. After an orgy of chocolate tasting, we adjourned to La Coupole, where we spent the afternoon assessing the compatibility of *foie gras* with Austrian Gewürztraminer and Kentucky bourbon with *île flottante*.

Something about the way those ladies had stood, heels rocked back on nonexistent riding boots, chins up as if looking out from under the brim of an invisible Stetson, suggested the kind of clothes they wore back home. So looking at Jesse Joe, I felt mainly déjà vu. From the ten-gallon hat, embroidered cowboy shirt, and string tie secured by a steer-skull–shaped bolo, to his stack-heeled lizard-skin boots, toe-capped in silver, he was dressed for the Country Music Hall of Fame. Almost as impressive were his hair and beard. Voluminous and powder white, they foamed from under his hat and exploded around his face like stuffing from a gutted mattress. He was Roy Rogers' unkempt uncle, Gene Autry's wild child, the bastard offspring of Big Nose Kate and Dirty Dingus Magee, Grizzly Adams reborn. By comparison, John Wayne looked like a Boston accountant.

"Saw on your website as how you hung out here," he said, looking around the café. "Thought I'd just take a chance and drop by."

"Of course. Good to see you."

The waiter materialized. *"Je vous écoute."*

"Uh, would you like something?" I said.

"Sure, I could see an eye-opener. Double scotch, water back."

The waiter's eyebrows climbed into his hairline. Whisky—at eleven o'clock in the morning? The French never drink hard liquor before lunch. It's exclusively a *digestif*, sipped after a meal, to settle the stomach. If they drink it before then, it's only as *grog Americain*, mixed with sugar and hot water. Returning, he carried the tray at arm's length, as if the glass were radioactive. Callaway downed half the shot at a swallow. On what little skin remained visible under the whiskers, a network of capillaries lit up like Christmas lights newly connected to the mains. Clearly Jesse Joe was no stranger to the hard stuff.

"Haven't been in Paris since . . . must be '99," he said. "Year I warmed up for Bob Seger."

"Oh, you're a musician?"

"Well . . . *yeah!*" Astonished by my ignorance, he put down his glass and frowned. "Jesse Joe *Callaway?*"

"I don't think . . ."

"Of Stinky and the Toadsuckers? Horny, Blue and Sandy Sue? Cathouse Herman's Famous Five?"

"Sorry . . ."

"You *hafta* know 'Ya Got Me Dancing in My Pants'! Five weeks at number one. It's on the soundtrack of *Truckstop Crapshoot III.*"

"Well, a lot of good music doesn't make it to this side of the Atlantic," I said hurriedly. "But tell me: why are you here this time? Playing somewhere?"

"No. I'm pretty well retired now." He sank the rest of the scotch and looked around for the waiter. "Got a little spread outside El Paso. Coupla hundred head. Nothing fancy." He leaned forward earnestly. "I mean, it's like my ol' daddy used to say—at our age, what do ya really need but tight pussy, loose shoes, and a warm place to shit?"

We meditated on this paternal wisdom in silence. Then he said, "But that's what I wanted to talk to you about. I know this guy . . ."

When I got home, I told Marie-Dominique about Callaway and his scheme. It wasn't the first time something similar had been suggested. Details varied, but my role didn't. He would bring groups from the United States. I would organize an itinerary, liaise with hotels, arrange transport, give orientation talks, translate, and deal with any minor problems. In return, I got half the profits, invariably described as munificent.

"What did you tell him?"

"Same as all the others."

Whenever people made these proposals, I always nodded and said, "Very interesting, just keep me up to date, we should talk some more, I'd like to see some figures." Mostly I never heard from them again. Occasionally there was an embarrassed email: "Didn't get the response we hoped for . . . slump in tourist spending . . . maybe next year . . ."

"I did do one thing a little different," I said. "Probably shouldn't have."

"What?"

"Well, he's a musician. He asked if there was anybody he should catch while he was in town."

She frowned. "Oh, you didn't!"

"Yes," I said, "I sent him to hear Gelenter."

She shook her head in disapproval. "John, you should be ashamed of yourself."

Part One

NIGHT 1:
SOUND

10

Blues in the Night

Without music, life would be a mistake.
FRIEDRICH NIETZSCHE

After dinner, I put on a CD of Chet Baker. If any music could get me in the mood to plan a sound walk, it was his ruefully murmured anthems to disappointment.

They're writing songs of love
But not for me . . .

From the start, I never considered that the music of a sound walk would be anything but jazz.

Between the ages of eleven and seventeen, when I lived in the featureless Australian outback, jazz was my solace and friend. Each weeknight at 9:00 p.m., I tuned my radio to the *Voice of America*. For the next hour, the rustle of the night was erased by the urbane voice of its long-time presenter, Willis Conover. Enunciating each syllable for an audience for whom English was not a first language, he guided us through this teasingly elusive music.

Since, on the far side of the world, French students heard the same broadcasts, existentialism evolved to Thelonious Monk, Miles Davis, and Charlie "Bird" Parker. Vian, Camus, Sartre, Barthes, de Beauvoir—all of us plugged into that same frail thread.

Jazz and philosophy are natural bedfellows. In 1949, someone introduced Parker to Jean-Paul Sartre at the Club Saint-Germain in Paris. "Parker told me about his wish to study harmony at the Paris Conservatoire," Sartre said. "We talked about modern music." When they parted, Parker said, "I'm very glad to have met you. I like your playing very much." An artist may improvise just as powerfully with words and ideas as with an instrument.

How often, talking to some French writer or artist of my generation, had their eyes lit up as I mentioned the music of those years. And one winter night, in a clinically bleak municipal hall by the Canal Saint-Martin, at a concert by the vocal trio Les Amuse-Gueules, I was astonished when they launched into an a cappella version of Monk's bebop classic "Well You Needn't."

You're talkin' so sweet well you needn't
You say you won't cheat well you needn't
You're tappin' your feet well you needn't
It's over now, it's over now.

I felt like a traveler in the most remote corner of the world who suddenly hears someone speaking his own language.

The French first heard real jazz during World War I, when bandleader James Reese Europe toured to entertain the troops. Former musical director to dancers Vernon and Irene Castle, Europe was both an accomplished musician and a natural leader. His sixty-five-member unit comprised singers, dancers, and comedians—all jazz performers and, to the astonishment of Europeans, all black.

Everyone in the band could read music, but white audiences preferred the illusion of spontaneity, so Europe's sidemen memorized their often intricate arrangements. Paradoxically, this convinced the French that playing jazz was a skill unique to black Americans. For whites to attempt it was regarded as unwise, even unnatural. African American musicians flocked to France. When local players protested, the government ordered bandleaders to employ five Frenchmen for every foreigner. Rather than deprive their patrons of *le jazz hot*, entrepreneurs paid French sidemen to sit in silence while the Americans performed.

But Paris truly became a jazz capital during World War II, despite the music having been declared *entartete*—decadent—by Hitler and even though most jazz musicians were black, Jewish, or Gypsy, races the Nazis were sworn to exterminate. Needing entertainment for its troops, the Paris *kommandantur* turned a blind eye when the cafés of Saint-Germain-des-Prés converted their caves into *boites de nuit* and installed jazz groups. Luftwaffe Oberleutnant Dietrich Schulz-Köhn, who signed the permits to perform, became known as "Doktor Jazz" or "The Swing Doctor." A jazz fan both before and after the war, he claimed to have joined the Nazi Party in order to protect his enormous record collection.

Django Reinhardt, France's foremost jazz musician (and a Gypsy) was in England in 1940, but he returned to occupied Paris and played there throughout the war. Django was nothing like his introspective music. A dandy, given to white suits and red shoes, a slick hairdo and a hairline moustache, he went everywhere by chauf-

Django Reinhardt

feured limousine, generally with a trashily dressed *poule* on his arm.

Once word got around that he was in town, local Gypsies converged on the theater, often carrying live chickens stolen en route. If there was no open fire backstage to roast them, they broke up furniture and lit one, often in the center of the room. Reinhardt's behavior exasperated his colleague, the fastidious violinist Stéphane Grappelli. "Django made me very angry," he said. "He drank every day. He came [to performances] with no guitar. I gave Django my money. I hated him many times. But when he played, I loved Django! Everyone loved Django. Even the Nazis loved Django!"

I've never quite adjusted to the fact that, during the

1940s and 1950s, the intersection of rue de Buci and rue de Seine, the domestic corner where I buy my apples and cheese, was one of the centers of the jazz world. In the late 1920s, Philippe Soupault dismissed it as "a crossroads which gives birth to a family of short narrow streets; not alleys but dark and full of bad smells." Fortunately the bohemian intellectuals and musicians who moved into the area didn't mind. Opposite where the Carrefour supermarket now stands, the Hôtel La Louisiane soon harbored a colony of American performers and international eccentrics.

In October 1943, Simone de Beauvoir moved in. "I'd never lodged anywhere that fulfilled my dreams as that place did," she said. "I would have happily stayed there for the rest of my life. At the other end of the corridor, Sartre had a tiny room where he lived in a state of asceticism that never ceased to shock his visitors: he didn't even have any books." Francophile editor and writer Cyril Connolly and his mistress, Jean Bakewell, shared the oval bedroom on the top floor. They kept ferrets and lemurs in their room, feeding them gobbets of raw horse liver. Leather harnesses fitted with little bells helped keep track of them.

Lester Young, Miles Davis, John Coltrane, and Charlie Parker all lived at the Louisiane. Filmmaker

Bertrand Tavernier celebrated those days in his 1986 movie *Round Midnight*, retelling the story of how young jazz fan Francis Paudras adopted burned-out pianist Bud Powell—replaced by tenor saxophonist Dexter Gordon in the film. Too poor to pay the cover charge at the Café du Marché, on the corner of rue de Buci and rue de Seine, Paudras crouched in the rain, straining to hear Powell's music seeping like perfume through a ventilation grille. When Powell came up for some air between sets, Paudras bought him a glass of wine. Their friendship saved Powell's life. He moved in with Paudras, who restored him, for a few years at least, to health and productivity. So much for the "cruel and insensitive" French.

11

Paris on Sea

Paris is a hard place to leave.
WILLA CATHER

When I moved to Paris from Los Angeles at the end of 1989, Marie-Dominique and I lived for a few months in her tiny apartment on Place Dauphine, on the Île de la Cité.

That studio was my decompression chamber. Like a diver ascending from the depths, I needed time to adjust to my new environment. It looked out on an archetypal Paris space, a small park with a grove of chestnut trees. André Breton called it "one of the most profoundly secluded places I know. Whenever I happen to be there, I feel the desire to go somewhere else gradually ebbing out of me. I have to struggle against myself to get free from a gentle, overinsistent, and, finally, crushing embrace."

Place Dauphine from our balcony

By the time we moved to rue de l'Odéon, free for the first time to enjoy the city in comfort, I found that, from the sixth floor, Paris was a different place.

In Place Dauphine, we belonged to the area. Our first-floor windows made us extras in its never-ending spectacle—especially if we stepped out of the shower before the curtains were drawn. Rue de l'Odéon was quite different. Here, Paris provided the show. Taking morning coffee on the balcony, I became just another spectator.

North, the gray turnip-like domes of Sacré-Coeur

crowned the butte of Montmartre. South, just beyond the Théâtre de l'Odéon, rose the foliage of the Luxembourg Gardens. Less than a kilometer to the east, the towers of Notre Dame floated on an ocean of metal roofs. On Sunday evenings, its bells—the bells of Quasimodo!—tolled solemnly over the city of François Villon. It wasn't hard to imagine turn-of-the-century criminal genius Fantômas, in evening dress and black domino mask, slipping into one of those dormer windows left so invitingly ajar, or oneself as the young man of Jacques Rivette's *Paris Nous Appartient—Paris Belongs to Us—* strolling across the roof of the Théâtre du Châtelet, just on the other side of the Seine, an iconic image for me from the moment it appeared in *Cahiers du Cinema*.

Rue de l'Odéon was so narrow that one could look straight into the apartments opposite. Curtains are rare in Paris. The instrument of privacy is the *persienne*, a wooden shutter that can be bolted in winter or when the apartment is empty, or half-closed to shade a room against the sun. But as nobody bothered much with *persiennes* once the weather turned warm, the apartments opposite were as open to us as the rooms in a doll's house. I could read the names on the books scattered around the floor of the apartment two floors down and watch the maids of our richer neighbors as they plumped the pillows of the beds every morning or spent early evenings laying the table for twelve in preparation for twice-weekly dinner parties.

Summer light streaming into our apartment emphasized the stresses and subsidences inflicted by two centuries of gravity. There wasn't a horizontal line or a flat plane anywhere. Rooms tapered, low ceilings intersecting window frames at odd angles. Floors rippled, dipped, and rose unexpectedly so that a rolling ball would zigzag for yards, coming to rest in a far corner as if tired of searching. Paris reversed entropy. Here, all things tended not to a condition of rest but to perpetual motion.

12

Raspberry and Rose Petals

Stay me with flagons, comfort me with apples;
for I am sick of love.

Song of Solomon 2:4–6, *King James Bible*

One morning, we woke to a new sound, a dull repeated thud that reverberated through the thick
walls, throbbing like a sick headache. When I took my
coffee out on the balcony, I saw that, almost overnight,
scaffolding had appeared on half a dozen buildings.
There were skips up and down the street, some of them
already filling with rubble.

Marie-Do joined me and took in the chaos without
surprise.

"August," she said, as if that explained everything.

Catholics call their important feasts "holy days of

The Paris plage

obligation." Even for the godless, however, the summer break is just as obligatory, ruled by an unspoken Eleventh Commandment: In August thou shalt *faire les vacances*.

From late July to early September, cafés, shops, and theaters crank down shutters and put up signs announcing *Congé Annuel*—annual vacation. Jackhammers rattle along empty boulevards like machine gun fire as cafés use downtime to install new bars and extra tables, preparing for their busiest season, the autumn and winter. For citizens unable to escape, the city covers a few hundred meters along the Seine with sand for the *Paris plage*—the Paris beach. For the deprived, however, it's more of a torment, a vision of the paradise from which they are barred.

Spending July and August in the village of Fouras—pronounced "Foo-rah"—on the Atlantic coast has become second nature to us, a kind of migration as unchanging as the equinoxes. But not to take Paris with us on vacation would be unthinkable. The British, the Americans, the Germans abandon their metropolitan habits when they go on holiday, but the Parisians, snaillike, carry their city with them. Each resort from Le Touquet to Juan-les-Pins becomes Paris on Sea.

Preparations commence with the end of the school year. Louise, who's studying in London, returns home. Her day begins around 11:00 a.m. Standing sleepily in the kitchen, she prepares a brunch of Krisprolls and herbal tea. Two hours later, she admits the first of a succession of friends with whom she retreats to her room for most of the afternoon, segueing into preparations for an evening around the clubs of the *grands boulevards*.

But even Louise puts social life on hold for August. "When are we going to Fouras?" is followed by "Can I invite some friends?" and then the ominous supplementary "How long will you be staying?"—a hint that, depending on her guest list, there might not be room for us. Following some tight-lipped negotiation and occasional shouts of *"J'en ai marre"*—I'm fed up—we establish our right to one bedroom but cede the rest to *les filles*.

Like a sleeper agent reactivated as a prelude to war, our *femme de ménage* in Fouras, Henriette, is alerted to the imminent invasion. During the rest of the year, she drops in periodically to check on the house, but in summer she's at work three days a week, mopping the tiles on the ground floor, sweeping the cedar floors upstairs, summoning a gardener to mow the ankle-deep grass of the lawn and trim the overgrown hedges that hide us from the street.

Propane tanks for the stove are replenished, last year's rice and pasta dumped from the larder. Liters of mineral water and tetra-packs of long-life milk accumulate in the cave. The other essentials she leaves to us, knowing we enjoy browsing markets for fresh-pressed olive oil, powder-like *fleur de sel* from the salt pans of Brouage, honey scented with wildflowers, wine from local cooperatives, decanted by the liter into plastic Evian bottles, and jams, homemade from whatever the maker has scavenged from end-of-season windfalls.

These jams are the sole source of friction between us and Henriette. We buy some from the lady in the market who sells tomatoes, basil, and eggs from her own garden. Others come from street markets. Hand-lettered labels detail the often outlandish mixtures of fruit that went into them—*abricot, framboise, pêche*. Some combinations—*bananes et petales de roses*— verge on the surrealist. A kiwi or mango in the blend justifies *fruits exotiques*. Some simply give up and say *fruits mixte*.

Henriette scorns these home productions. Who knows what goes into them? And what's wrong with factory-produced *confitures* such as the popular line made by Bonne Maman? We justify our enthusiasm as part of that urge to reconnect with our heritage. Eating them reminds us of times when decisions were simpler and choices less various. The more authentic the objects surrounding us during the *vacances*, the more powerful the impression of simpler days. Big food companies have been quick to exploit this. Shrewdly, Bonne Maman jams copy the octagonal jars used by country house-wives. Their labels use imitation handwriting, and all their packaging—jams, cake mixes, biscuits—imitates the red-and-white gingham with which amateurs tradi-tionally wrap the lids of their jars.

Our holiday enthusiasm for the antique extends even into the lavatory. It's novel to yank a chain rather than push a button, and no chill vinyl seat can compare to warm, well-worn oak. In Fouras, we even embrace the antique in our choice of lavatory deodorant. Instead of aerosol air freshener, we burn *papier d'Arménie*— Armenian paper. Colored slips—purple, orange, deep green—are torn from a booklet, set alight, and dropped into a saucer, where they smolder with smoke that smells like vanilla but is actually benzoin resin from the Styrax tree. Even the Armenian inventors no longer use this, but to us its very obsolescence makes it attractive.

In most country markets, someone is usually selling locally made soap, heavy, sharp-edged, semitranslucent blocks, odorous with their primary component, olive oil. We lug home a few slabs and, virtuously, use them next time we shower—no easy task, since they produce about as much lather as a brick and leave one coated with oil, smelling like a badly dressed salad. Generally a block survives only until the first time it slips from your fingers and lands on a toe. After that, it's demoted to the edge of the sink, to squat like a cubist toad, yellow-green, a silent rebuke to our foamy store-bought Dove and Palmolive.

Mental time-traveling is at its most potent in *brocantes*. Most of the year, Parisians throng such electronic-goods stores as Darty, insisting on washing machines or microwaves so technically advanced one needs a science degree to understand the manual. On holiday, however, they crowd into flea markets that convene in village squares and football grounds. Scrambling under tables and ferreting in cartons, they'll coo with delight over chipped tureens or dented lamp bases, reverently installing their finds in the trunks of their Alfa-Romeos and Mercedes.

13

Eating Well Is the Best Revenge

Seating themselves on the greensward, they eat while the corks fly and there is talk, laughter and merriment, and perfect freedom, for the universe is their drawing room and the sun their lamp. Besides, they have appetite, Nature's special gift, which lends to such a meal a vivacity unknown indoors, however beautiful the surroundings.

JEAN ANTHELME BRILLAT-SAVARIN, on eating outdoors

Over the years, my role in August has settled down to that of cook. In return for feeding the house, I'm excused all exposure to the sun. From the shade of the big pear tree in the garden, I watch, book in hand, as Marie-Dominique, her mother Claudine, and Louise and her friends leave for the beach.

Until lunchtime, I'm free to read, enjoy another cup of coffee, and plan the day's menus.

Not that they need much planning. I compile them after I've seen what's on offer, particularly in the ancient stone fish market. To step out of the stinging sun into its moist chill is to enter a different sensorium. The slap of flip-flops on the wet floor echoes through the building like a definition of cool. Closer to individual stalls, sounds contract to the barely audible—the slither of live eels, a clacking of claws from armored crabs, the skitter of gray-green baby shrimp, twitching six inches deep in a box.

A circuit of the stalls gives me a sense of possibilities. Much as I'm tempted by freshly dredged scallops and some plump langoustines, I halt at the seller who offers a *méli-mélo* of mixed fish, cut in small cubes. I buy a kilo, to her obvious surprise. Why would I, usually a finicky client for whole turbot or Saint Pierre, want these leftovers of salmon, tuna, and sea bass? Mostly they sell to lazy cooks who will use them as a shortcut to a cliché *bourride* or *soupe de poissons*.

I try to explain that these pieces, mixed with chopped red onions and herbs, copious lime juice, and fresh green chili, will, after an hour in the fridge, transform themselves into ceviche. She isn't impressed. This far from

Paris, few support the exotic. I recognize her silent rebuke; if it was good enough for Napoleon, it should be good enough for you.

Fouras's main *halle*, high and long as an aircraft hangar, has everything else I need for lunch: limes, red onions, broad-leaved basil, coriander, fat heavy tomatoes, and fresh lettuce. For dessert, I'm tempted by melons from nearby Chataillon, still crusted with dirt from the garden where they were picked that morning.

I ask Louise what sense she feels is best represented by Fouras. "Touch," she says instantly.

I know what she means. Here in the south, one encounters things never felt in Paris: sand in the bedclothes; the dark slickness of a bay leaf fresh-plucked, glossy, flexible, aromatic. And melons still moist, and rough with the earth of the field where they were grown.

I briefly contemplate melon as dessert but decide on a Fouras specialty: *jonchée*.

To make *jonchée*—pronounced "John-shay"—dairy farmers add rennet to full-cream milk. It separates into watery whey and soft white curds: the "curds and whey" that Little Miss Muffet eats in the nursery rhyme. Collecting the curds, which resemble jellied cream, they roll them in a mat woven from reeds—also called *jonchée*. As the mat unrolls, the curds tumble out as a fluted cylinder, to be served with a little of the whey flavored with almond essence, and a sprinkling of sugar or a spoonful of jam. As *jonchée* can't be frozen or preserved and is too fragile to travel, it's that ideal of locavores, a product that must be eaten within sight of its source.

When the beach party troops back, flushed, sandy, and starving, we sit down to lunch under the pear tree. Looking round the table, I try to relate these chic young women, now lawyers, doctors, and venture capitalists, to the gawky teens I first met ten years ago. Back then, they frowned at anything more exotic than noodles and filled up on bread, cheese, and salad rather than take a chance on stuffed eggplant or chicken biryani. Now they scarf up my ceviche, nachos, and fresh salsa almost before they're served.

"Gourmet food like this, down here," marvels one, taking a third helping. "Who'd have thought?"

Is there any greater encouragement to a cook than appetite? My safe choice for dinner—salad Niçoise or a quiche—goes out the window. Now I'm thinking Thai chicken curry with coconut milk, lemongrass, and basil.

14

Time and Tide

It bothers people—friends, I mean—that I spend
every August in Paris. They think it is unhealthy,
surely lonely, probably eccentric. The truth is that I
prefer being in a city, all the time, more and more,
and "city" means Paris. I am frequently offered
an airy room in a country house, in Normandy, in
Brittany, and sometimes the house itself. I am as-
sured that I would be able to work in peace, that no
one would ever bother me, that I could just turn up
for meals. Thank you, no.

MAVIS GALLANT

Life in Fouras pulses lazily to the two-beat rhythm of the tides. Every twelve hours, water from the Atlantic surges into the estuary and brings to life the beaches, bays, and moorings that line the bay and riverbanks. Each house has a leaflet giving times of high and low water, and it's consulted religiously. As the tide advances, the lanes fill with people hustling seaward, determined not to waste a minute of high water. For three or four hours, kids splash in a modest surf, sunbathers discreetly expose to the sun breasts pale as scoops of *glace vanille*, families gather under huge umbrellas, while up on the esplanade the less active drowse in cafés and bars until the water recedes and the town shuts up for lunch.

As the hour of high tide moves with the moon, a little later each day, mealtimes lag. We eat lunch at three and dinner when we should be in bed. I protest, but Fouras is all about the beach, and a cook can no more defy the tide than King Canute, who rebuked his courtiers by demonstrating that, no matter how forcefully he ordered the ocean to recede, it ignored him.

On the last Saturday of my stay, Claudine, my mother-in-law, invited Louise and me to lunch at a *crêperie* on the esplanade. Though it is a kind gesture, I recognized an element of self-interest. At ninety-three, she's uncomfortable at our crowded summer table in the company of young people, some speaking English she doesn't understand. After one long passage of Franglais, she muttered, "I understood two words of that—'television' and 'cheese.' " By paring down her companions to Louise and me, she hoped for conversation rather than cacophony.

Since last summer, the *crêperie* had gone Australian. Aboriginal-style drawings of kangaroos and lizards decorated the windows, and pancakes were named for Australian towns. I scanned the menu, wondering if, in its embrace of antipodean cuisine, they were offering authentic Aussie fillings—bogong moths, perhaps, or witchetty grubs—but the makeover was merely cosmetic. They still served paper-thin slightly crisp pancakes of *sarrazin*—buckwheat—folded over eggs, cheese, or charcuterie, eaten with dry cider, served, in the tradition of Normandy, in bowls.

I opted for the Canberra, puzzlingly filled with merguez, the North African sausage spiced with red pepper. As Canberra, the political capital, is also the center of corruption and graft, I instructed them to slip in an additional egg.

"Why Australian?" I asked the waitress.

"The owner has two brothers living there," she said.

It was a flimsy pretext, but a shrewd one. While the French admire aspects of Britain and the United States, there's too much shared history for any real rapprochement. Australia, however, has a clean slate.

That's not to say the average French person knows much about the world's largest island. Just as, to them, the American west is inhabited entirely by Native Americans and cowboys, Australia is exclusively the domain of its aboriginal people. The Australian embassy in Paris seems to have an exhibition of tribal paintings year-round, and the nearby Musée du Quai Branly includes whole galleries of art and craft work.

As Louise chatted to Claudine while we waited for our crepes, I looked across the now-shallow bay toward a horizon as smearily undefined as a landscape by Australia's preeminent artist of the 1940s and 1950s, Sidney Nolan. During World War II, the army exiled Nolan to the Wimmera, the flat wheat country of Victoria. Deserting, he hid out for a year and then sailed for England, to become famous for paintings of those limitless plains, inhabited by the ghost of their most famous outlaw, Ned Kelly, a lumbering shape in black homemade armor hammered from ploughshares.

Nolan discovered something I later noticed myself. Asked what inspired the Ned Kelly paintings, he said, "Rousseau—and sunlight." He meant Henri Rousseau, the postimpressionist primitive who painted only on Sundays, since he worked weekdays collecting tolls, a job that earned him the nickname *Le Douanier,* the customs officer.

Australian light defeated most painters. English light was for us returning exiles what the madeleine was for Proust: a key that unlocked our past. No longer squinting into blue-white glare, we saw our native country with new insight, even affection. Reticent about praising our native soil while we lived there, we sometimes became, as expatriates, nostalgic for it, even sentimental. "I say ours is a bitter heritage," wrote the Australian novelist Randolph Stow, "but that is not to run it down." Another expatriate, T. S. Eliot, an American who relocated in Europe, put it even better.

We shall not cease from exploration
And the end of all our exploring
Will be to arrive where we started
And know the place for the first time.

The French, for whom no country could be even a fraction as interesting as their own, wonder if we foreigners really have the stamina and commitment to live here. Life for the newcomer can seem a succession of pettifogging linguistic puzzles, pointless social usages, and mindless bureaucracies, throughout which the French watch narrowly, waiting for our tempers to crack. "Aha!" they say as we throw the latest government form to the floor and stamp on it, "We knew you weren't sincere. Secretly, you despise us." An American journalist, interviewing a French starlet, found her so charming he almost believed she was sexually interested in him—until he confessed that he hadn't seen a couple of her films. Her manner became arctic. "You are like all the rest," she pouted. "And to think I believed you were doing this out of love!"

Even my adoptive family took its time deciding I'd come to stay. In their minds, Marie-Dominique was already cast as glamorous and footloose *Tante* DouDou. Always off to Africa or America on some journalistic project, scattering doleful lovers in her wake, she'd be far too busy and independent to marry. My abrupt appearance in her life was puzzling enough, our marriage and the birth of Louise even more so. Their expectations frustrated, my potential in-laws regarded me with suspicion. I could have been packed off back to America or Australia, smarting from wounded vanity, instead of relaxing here, enjoying the comfort of my family, in the great good place. Fortunately, however, I married into a family of academics, painters, journalists, and educators, none of whom could cook. By the time my second French Christmas came around and Claudine asked me to cook dinner for twenty, I knew I had become indispensable.

15

Spending a Centime

For this relief much thanks.
SHAKESPEARE, *Hamlet*

I n leading walks, I've noticed that, although certain
subjects, seldom literary, are never far from a visitor's mind, most are reticent about showing an interest.

Foremost among them is sex.

Salvador Dalí, on his first unsupervised trip out of
Spain in 1929, took a cab directly from the railway station to the city's most famous brothel, Le Chabanais,
and demanded an instant erotic education. Madrid had
just as many bordellos as Paris, some as splendid as Le
Chabanais, but those of Paris were widely recognized
to offer that little something extra. Young Salvador was

not disappointed. After a few hours in a room reserved for voyeurs and well supplied with peepholes, he reeled into the street, having seen, he said, quite enough to furnish his fantasies for the rest of his life.

Brothels may have given way to Internet escort services, but the illusion of Paris, city of love, persists. Summer and winter, you can usually find a Japanese photographer hard at work on the Pont Alexandre III, the bridge that joins the foot of the Champs-Élysées with the park in front of the Hôtel des Invalides. He's snapping bare-shouldered Japanese brides and tail-coated grooms as they pose against a background of the seventeenth-century façade of Les Invalides. Why not London's Tower Bridge or Berlin's Brandenburg Gate? Because, they explain earnestly, Paris is the city of love. Later, the same couples sit in a café, indifferent to one another but busily texting details of their romantic honeymoon to friends back to Tokyo.

Certain clients perk up when I mention that a narrow building near the corner of rue Mazarine and rue de Buci had been, before such establishments were outlawed in 1946, a *maison close*, or brothel. Whorehouses favored slender premises with a single entrance. The madame, stationed on the top floor and using a system of mirrors on each landing, could watch who came in and out—something demonstrated to me by screenwriter Jean-Claude Carrière, whose home in Pigalle is a converted *bordel*.

Just opposite Église Saint-Sulpice I point out a similarly narrow establishment that catered to priests. Having sinned, guilty clerics had only to cross the street to confess and be forgiven. For good measure, I'd add that Henry Miller, as well as patronizing a number of brothels, wrote the text for the brochures published by one of the most prestigious, Montparnasse's Le Sphinx, and was paid to steer friends into its gilded air-conditioned salon and mirrored bedrooms.

All this is too much for some clients. One sidled up and murmured, "Um, I don't suppose such places still exist?" Another asked if I knew anyone who gave "private French lessons." I sent him to a poet friend who taught as a sideline, but when I asked about their progress, she said frostily, "His idea of irregular verbs was a little too irregular."

After sex, the second more common subject of conversation is . . . well, Roget's *Thesaurus* lists its synonyms better than I can. Crap, poop, dung, excrement, feces, manure, night soil . . . or, to the French, *l'ordure*.

After rude waiters, no aspect of Paris life receives so much negative publicity as the prevalence of doggie doo-doo. One would think from some descriptions that the stuff lies in drifts, like snow after a blizzard. In fact, there never was a great deal of it, and the amount is dwindling. The reason is less sanitary than financial. Parisians used to keep Great Danes, Saint Bernards, and Russian wolfhounds in their apartments, but the high cost of feeding them has driven them to downsize to Yorkshire terriers. Nor does one see as many of those skittish breeds such as the dalmatian and poodle, so inclined to leave their malodorous souvenirs wherever it suited them. The choice of a pet, once a matter of class—to have a dog, the larger the better, signified prestige—is now more one of style; can your *toutou* fit into a handbag and remain quietly at your feet when you take him into a restaurant?

Three or four times a year, at the top of our street, a film crew cordons off Place de l'Odéon, in front of the imposingly colonnaded Théâtre de l'Odéon (built 1783), to shoot a period melodrama. Locals watch amused as actors and actresses in spotless crinolines and gleaming boots stroll across the cobbles—something they never did in real life.

At the time of Britain's Henry VIII, only half of

Crossing a Paris gutter, nineteenth century

Paris's streets were paved. The rest were bare earth: dusty and uneven when dry, muddy swamps after rain. Open drains carried the runoff. Rubbish and filth were everywhere. Our street, rue de l'Odéon, built around 1760, was the first in the city to have a sidewalk. Until Napoleon III transformed Paris in the 1870s, only the poor walked. The rich went everywhere on horseback or by carriage. Trotting right through the front gate of a building into the courtyard, they left their animals with the stable boys and took the stairs to the first floor. Their feet never touched the ground.

Even if canine truffles decorated every modern sidewalk, their quantity would scarcely rival the manure left by all those horses, not to mention the cows, goats, sheep, and chickens which, until the 1920s, Parisian householders kept in their courtyards. One sympathizes with the movie directors who omit the filth. It's hard to show La Rochefoucauld crafting an epigram just as his boot sinks ankle-deep into horseshit.

Even worse was human excrement. The British word "loo," for toilet, may derive from the warning *Gardez l'eau*—Look out for the water!—that preceded the emptying of a chamber pot out the window. Even in the eighteenth century, this was thought vulgar. The more fastidious patronized the men with leather buckets who cruised the city's fashionable avenues, carrying tentlike cloaks to drape around clients as they used them.

Buckets gave way to a kind of rolling privy on wheels. City ordinances required that these keep moving, occupied or not, which must have made relieving oneself a hazardous matter as the cabinet jolted over cobbles. In time, the government accepted that some functions require tranquility and introduced the semipublic *vespasi-enne,* or pissoir. Barely obscured by metal screens that began above the knee and ended below the neck, men—but only men—could relieve themselves on the busiest street. Despite the smell and minimal concessions to privacy, one lady remarked tartly that "there cannot be an Englishwoman exploring Paris who would not, at some time, have shelved her hygienic objections if only such provision had been made for her."

Writers, expatriate or otherwise, have little to say about sanitation. An exception was Henry Miller, who positively relished defecation. To him, all human functions affirmed life. "I love everything that flows," he wrote. "Rivers, sewers, lava, semen, blood, bile, words, sentences. I love the amniotic fluid when it spills out of the bag. I love the kidney with its painful gall-stones, its gravel and what-not; I love the urine that pours out scalding and the clap that runs endlessly; I love the words of hysterics and the sentences that flow on like dysentery and mirror all the sick images of the soul." In particular, he patronized a pissoir in the Luxembourg Gardens that permitted him to pee while peering over an adjoining fence at families enjoying a picnic.

For two hundred years, French lavatories were of the awkward and unsavory "Turkish" type. One squatted over an open hole and risked having one's feet inundated by the flush. In his 1966 survey, *Guide Porcelaine to the Loos of Paris*, sanitary scholar Jonathan Routh called them "crouchers," though an Australian came up with a more vivid term, describing the process of using them as "kangaroo-ing." Though doctors insist that squatting is more natural and healthy than sitting, the croucher has few friends. In the early 1970s, while I waited on the seafront at Ostend for the ferry to Britain, a busload of American college girls pulled up. One darted into the sanitation block and popped out a few seconds later to shout ecstatically, "Real toilets!" One more reason to visit Au Bon Saint Pourçain, the tiny restaurant on rue Servandoni, just by the church of Saint-Sulpice, was the insistence of François, the owner, on preserving his traditional WC—another touch of authenticity, along with the menu chalked on the slate and the complementary glass of wine from his own village.

Even after Paris had sewers, few apartments included toilets or bathrooms. A building of fifty or sixty tenants might have only three or four lavatories, all on the landings of the main staircase, and seldom cleaned. When Parisians congregated in cafés, they did so mainly to enjoy the intellectual ambiance and the company of their peers, but the washrooms were an added incentive, supervised as they were by a *madame pipi* who not only kept them clean but also, for a few centimes, provided soap and a hand towel.

Pissoirs disappeared in the 1980s. As well as being smelly and embarrassing, they attracted both prostitutes and exhibitionists. The automated self-service cabinets that replaced them offer good service when they work—which is seldom. It's easier to visit a café, buy an *express* at the *zinc*, then enjoy the privacy and cleanliness of its *petit coin*—the "little corner."

At times, that experience can be as transcendental as even Henry Miller might have wished: in the art deco luxury of the toilets under La Coupole, for instance, or the tile, brass, and varnished elegance of Brasserie Vagenende on boulevard Saint-Germain. And yet, reading Routh's *Loos of Paris* today, one almost feels nostalgic for the era of sanitary adventurism in the Paris of General de Gaulle. Routh gives the search for a loo an Edwardian sense of hazard and discovery, making it sound like an expedition into darkest Africa. Seeking relief in the Paris Opéra, he found a custodian who, for 50 centimes, sold him a ticket and gave him a key to the toilet, with complex directions on how to find it. When Routh finally got there, it was well worth the walk, though not for the reasons one might imagine.

It had a red fitted carpet, 1 toilet, 1 basin, and one other tiny toilet for the smaller person. Also in the room, a large cupboard, which, because there was a slight shortage of paper beside my toilet, I opened in search of more. I found very much more inside; ancient files of the Opéra with original letters from the family Strauss, hand-written scores of goodness knows who. I feel it a pity if, during any subsequent period of paper shortage, a less scrupulous toileter than myself were to put these irreplaceable documents to the use for which the room is designed, and I recommended to the Musée authorities to lock their cupboard in order to remove the temptation.

Paris pissoir, c. 1900

16

Help the Poor Struggler

One, two! One two! And through and through
The vorpal blade went snicker-snack!
He left it dead, and with its head
He went galumphing back.

LEWIS CARROLL, *Through the Looking-Glass*

At times, the movable feast of Paris carries one in strange, even sinister directions. When I pause at a nondescript house in the Cour du Commerce Saint-André to explain that it was here Doctor Joseph-Ignace Guillotin perfected the instrument of execution that bore his name, I expect the occasional grimace, even a shudder. One client, however, a pale young man with something of Norman Bates about him, showed more interest. Lagging behind the group, he took out a notebook.

"Is the guillotine still in use?"

"Oh, no," I said. "The last execution was in 1977. France abandoned capital punishment in 1981."

He made a note. "And where did they . . . er . . . ? "

"Well, it depended. Usually at the Santé prison."

He licked the end of his pencil. "How do you spell that? "

Why the guillotine became, literally overnight, France's official method of execution illustrates the advice to be careful what you wish, since you may get it.

Dr. Guillotin, far from favoring capital punishment, was a vigorous opponent. He loathed the way executions had become a public show, with mobs, including children, gathering to watch felons hanged, burned at the stake, broken on the wheel, or hacked to death with blunt swords or axes. That was only for the poor, however. The wealthy often bribed the executioner to drug them, knock them out, or even, occasionally, kill someone in their place. This tradition survived in Britain right up to the abolition of capital punishment. A member of the House of Lords convicted of a capital crime could elect to be hanged with a rope of slippery silk, not rough hemp.

Guillotin argued for the abolition of capital punishment on the grounds that its methods contravened the equality provision of the Revolution's motto *Liberté*,

Égalité, Fraternité. Surely every criminal, rich or poor, should be killed in the same way. The Assemblée Nationale accepted his argument and set up a committee that included Guillotin to develop an alternative. Guillotin was delighted. Once a machine did the job, he reasoned, executions would become boringly repetitive and the whole practice would wither away.

The group found designs for a decapitation device used in Italy and Scotland and took them to a maker of harpsichords named Tobias Schmidt. He created a pro-

totype, testing it out first on sheep, then on a highway-
man. It worked perfectly. But when Guillotin reported
his success to the Assemblée, he was a little too enthusiastic. "With my machine," he boasted in a widely reported speech, "you feel no more than a breeze on the
back of your neck."

This was a boast too far, and it backfired. People
came to see the device in action, and liked what they
saw. Every town in France wanted one; Schmidt became
rich, particularly during the mass slaughter of aristo-
crats, intellectuals, and clergy known as The Terror.

Though he hadn't invented the guillotine, Guillotin's name became attached to it. A Dr. J. M. V. Guillotin from Lyon was executed, sparking the rumor that
the device's inventor had also become its victim. Plenty
of people would have liked to see him decapitated as
their friends and relatives had been, but vanity saved the
doctor. So many people, particularly foreigners, associated him with the machine and, what was almost worse,
mispronounced it, calling the instrument "Madame la
Guillotine," that he changed his name.

Having embraced the guillotine, France was reluc-
tant to let it go. Until capital punishment ended, it was
the sole civil method of execution; the military retained
the firing squad. While prison authorities in most coun-

tries remove the theatrical element from executions, decapitations in France were positively flamboyant. Until 1939, they took place in public. Someone snatched a film of that particular termination, so thereafter they were held in prison yards. People with apartments or houses overlooking such places hired out their rooms to sensation seekers who watched, trembling with excitement, as the prisoner was led out.

By tradition, the condemned was carried to the site in a horse-drawn cart lit by a lantern and saluted with a flourish of sabers from the military guard before mounting the scaffold. The executioner also had the right to wear a red flower behind his ear or in his buttonhole and to *tutoyer* the prisoner, addressing him not as *vous* but *tu*, as one would a friend.

Beforehand, the machine was tested with a bundle of straw with the same resistance as the neck. The prisoner, dressed in shirtsleeves, was then strapped face-down to a plank and slid into place. A board with a half-moon-shaped gap, called a *lunette*, was swung down to hold his head, and the blade fell. An instant later, the body rolled sideways into a wicker basket while the executioner's assistant held up the head by the hair to show justice had been down.

This particular ritual collected a wealth of mythology. At the execution of Charlotte Corday for murdering another revolutionary leader, Jean-Paul Marat, a carpenter named Legros who was repairing the guillotine grabbed the head and, curious to test a theory that the brain remained alive after separation, slapped its cheeks as he held it up. Witnesses reported an expression of "unequivocal indignation" on Corday's face. For taking such a liberty with a woman of good reputation, murderess or not, Legros was jailed for three months and barely escaped with his life.

Much as the crowd loved the spectacle of a good execution, the authorities also treated it as a guilty secret, disassembling the guillotine after each use and storing the parts in a secret location. Putting it back together and testing it was time-consuming. As timbers warped and pieces disappeared, it could take weeks to reassemble the device, with much use of spirit levels and plumb bobs to make sure it was completely true.

In common with the British hangman but unlike those in the United States, the French executioner was a private individual and the job was a family business. Two families, the Sansons and the Deiblers, performed every execution between 1792 and 1981. Traditionally anonymous, the executioner was always referred to as "Monsieur de Paris." Between executions, he pursued an ordinary profession. Britain's longtime hangman, Albert Pierrepoint, ran a pub called, ghoulishly, Help the Poor Struggler. Most French executioners were discreet but Henri-Clément Sanson, who had the job in the middle of the nineteenth century, was an exception. An alcoholic, he raised money by giving public demonstrations, cutting off the heads of sheep. Before the authorities could execute the next criminal, they had to redeem the guillotine from where Sanson had pawned it. They let him supervise that execution, and then they fired him.

17

The Sense of a Sacrifice

Sometimes I'm invited places to kind of brighten up a dinner table like a musician who'll play the piano after dinner, and I know you're not really invited for yourself. You're just an ornament.

MARILYN MONROE

ave you ever heard," asked my sister-in-law, Caroline, "of a woman named Kitty Carlisle Hart?"

As Caroline headed the Paris campus of a major stateside university, we occasionally found ourselves discussing obscure aspects of American culture. Few of them, however, related to such minor show business personalities as the longtime panelist of the TV game show *To Tell the Truth* and widow of *My Fair Lady* producer Moss Hart.

"What can I tell you?"

"Ah, so you know who she is?"

Kitty Carlisle Hart wearing fronds—but little else in
Murder at the Vanities.

"Better than that. I've seen her naked. Well, near
enough, anyway."

Caroline sounded startled. "I'm not sure I need to
know that much," she said. "She's on our board of re-
gents. She'll be here next week, with a group of alumni.
I've been planning their itinerary. We need to make a
good impression."

"What did you have in mind?"

"Well, I thought a guided tour of the usual sights—Tour Eiffel, Arc de Triomphe . . . that sort of thing."

"The others might enjoy that, but not Madame Hart. As I remember, she graduated from the Sorbonne."

"Really?"

"Began her show business career in opera. Even sang *Carmen*—in French, I presume."

"That changes things. What *would* she enjoy?"

"In my experience," I said, "a good dinner seldom disappoints."

We think of the French as preferring simple food, carefully prepared and eaten in discreet surroundings. Let tourists patronize the chic bistros with their brass fittings and windows of colored glass, their white-aproned waiters and multiple-choice menus. The locals, we assume, are happiest dining on a few simple dishes prepared with care and craft, using ingredients harvested within sight of the kitchen's back door.

While this is generally true, the French, given the chance, will eat hugely, and with a gusto seldom seen in Anglo-Saxon cultures. The tradition of the *festin*, or feast, is enshrined in the culture. Such stories as Isak Dinesen's *Babette's Feast*, about a nineteenth-century Parisian refugee chef who shows her appreciation to the pious Norwegian community that sheltered her by preparing them a gourmet dinner, celebrate the transcendental pleasures of a massive meal enjoyed with friends. Uniquely, the practice even has its own word, or at least a suffix. Adding *-ade* to some delicacy—*sardinade, langoustinade*—signifies a public gathering to consume it in quantity. Excess is the most savory of sauces. As the writer Colette said of her favorite culinary indulgence, "If I can't have too many truffles, I don't want any."

Such feasts almost always take place in the countryside, in communities one would not think of as prosperous. The less wealthy the culture, the greater the effort it makes to produce a respectable feast. Jews went hungry but saved the fatted calf and the paschal lamb for roasting on a holy day. In that first bitter winter in the New World, the Pilgrims ate as lavishly as they could. At a Hawaiian luau, an entire pig, slow-roasted with yams and plantains, fed the tribe. In France, entire villages gather to roast an ox, gorge on the basil-flavored vegetable soup called pistou, or share an aioli—steamed fish and vegetables eaten with fiery garlic mayonnaise.

In each case, there is the sense of a sacrifice: of eating to celebrate the possibility of doing so. Such cheap foodstuffs as rice, potatoes, and pasta lend themselves to being consumed in quantity and shared with the entire family, even the community. It's prosperity that brings the arrogance of small portions. As incomes rise, grease and starch disappear, replaced by fatless protein, a few spoonfuls of green vegetables, a delicately sculpted potato—food prepared with an eye more to appearance than gratification. In one of the most telling details in Giuseppe di Lampedusa's novel *The Leopard*, his portrait of the Sicilian aristocracy on the eve of the Risorgimento, the bourgeoisie invited to dine with the Prince of Salina relax visibly when the meal they're served is not, as they fear, delicate dishes in the French style but deep pies filled with macaroni, liver, kidney, and sausages, all slippery with fat: the diet of the peasantry to which they still, in their guts, belong.

The continental tradition of the "good feed" also flourished in Australia, even in the country town where I was brought up. No matter how tough the times, organizers of a barn dance or "social" always found a way to provide supper for fifty or sixty people. They simply added to the announcement in the local paper the simple phrase "Ladies a Plate"; in other words, "We supply the premises and the band. You supply the food." Each woman brought a plate of sandwiches, cakes, sausage rolls; all, that is, except the occasional newcomer who took the request literally and arrived with just a naked plate.

After debating the options for feeding twenty wealthy New Yorkers, all fussy about their diets, Caroline booked a private room at La Pérouse. It was a shrewd choice. Since 1766, this restaurant overlooking the Seine on the Quai des Grands Augustins has purveyed a style of food and service most of us never dream of. When vegans and vegetarians wish to terrify their children, they take them on their knee and read from its menu. Before they've even reached the crawfish ravioli in Chantilly cream flavored with Hennessy cognac, let alone the chicken breast with hazelnut crust in a foie gras sauce, the most recalcitrant delinquent is begging for broccoli.

Even more impressively, we had been given one of the most richly decorated and gilded rooms in the restaurant. In calling it La Boussole—the compass—the restaurant paid tribute to Jean-François de La Pérouse, sent off in 1788 by Louis XVI in two ships, the *Astrolabe* and the *Boussole*, to circumnavigate the globe. He never returned. Louis's last question as he stood in the shadow of the guillotine in 1793 was, "Is there any news of Monsieur de La Pérouse?" He died without knowing that both ships had perished five years before on the reefs of Vanikoro in the Solomon Islands.

Given the public relations significance of the event,

I was flattered when Caroline invited me to the dinner but not deluded that I wouldn't be expected to sing for my supper. The food might be important, but so was the ambiance and, above all, the conversation. "Everything connected with dinner-giving has an almost sacramental importance in France," wrote American novelist Edith Wharton. "The quality of the cooking comes first; but, once this is assured, the hostess's chief concern is that the quality of the talk shall match it."

It seemed the conversation would be my responsibility—something confirmed as we waited at the top of the stairs for Madame Hart and her guests.

"Is there anything in particular you'd like me to do?" I asked.

"Just talk to Madame Hart," Caroline replied. "None of us would know what to say."

I felt a momentary qualm, since there wasn't much *to* say. As celebrities go, Kitty Carlisle was barely second string. Following some minor success in opera, she drifted to Hollywood, where her career peaked in 1935 as love interest to the Marx Brothers in *A Night at the Opera*. In 1946, she married Moss Hart, to become a Broadway hostess, game show personality, socialite, and fundraiser for worthy causes in the arts.

Would it be wise, I wondered, to confess that I admired her almost entirely on account of her first film, an obscure 1934 mystery called *Murder at the Vanities*?

Watching the frail woman mounting the stairs toward us, surrounded by men and women only slightly less venerable, I marveled at her vitality. Though a trifle unsteady on her feet, she looked spry for ninety-three. I knew she still toured in her one-woman show—not for the money, since Moss Hart died rich, but, as she confessed to me later that evening, to feel for just a few more hours the warmth of the limelight.

The evening didn't begin well. As she offered her fragile hand and the polite but weary smile of the public woman, I sensed the fatigue of a week—indeed a lifetime—expended on politesse. Been here, she seemed to say, done that. The rest of the party appeared less like friends than a supporting cast, chosen for their colorlessness, the better to show her off. They wandered into the dining room, silently studying the decor or impassively peering out the front windows at the gun-metal waters of the Seine: extras awaiting their cue. Most looked as if they'd be happier at home in front of the TV with their slippers and a cup of hot chocolate. Extreme measures were called for.

"What do you think we should do?" Caroline murmured.

"I could say something."

"Why don't you do that."

Taking a deep breath, I tapped on a wineglass with a fork to quiet the conversation, introduced myself, then went on. "Tonight, I've achieved a lifelong ambition . . ."

I was barely out of my teens when I saw *Murder at the Vanities*. Television was new to Australia, and entirely in black and white. Even to possess a set was exceptional. A significant proportion of the population, fanatically loyal to radio, believed that the set, even when dark, acted as an eye, recording everything they did and transmitting it to Security Central. People preferred sets with wooden doors that closed over the screen. Others kept it draped with a sheet.

Hungry for content, broadcasters bought the libraries of Hollywood studios and structured their schedules mostly around old movies. Care might go into choosing the films for prime time, but after midnight an assistant simply took the next can of film from the shelf and put it into the telecine. As prints tended to be grouped alphabetically by filmmaker, one might, in the course of a week, see five or six consecutive films by the same director—an ad hoc course in film appreciation that ignited my lifelong enthusiasm for Hollywood in the 1930s.

Even among the miscellany of gangster films, westerns, and musicals, however, *Murder at the Vanities* stood out. As phony as a celluloid hibiscus, it washed up in the early hours and seized my attention instantly. Set backstage at *Earl Carroll's Vanities*, a Broadway revue famous for lightly dressed showgirls, it was a message in a bottle from a world as remote from my experience as Egypt of the pharaohs.

Every scene, like cheap perfume, carried a whiff of those few gaudy years before Hollywood imposed a code of self-censorship that forbade everything from navels to knuckle-dusters. Nude girls, pale as lilies, coyly cupped their breasts and reclined in poses straight from the art deco pattern book. A boyish Duke Ellington, black hair and pearly teeth gleaming, conducted "Ebony Rhapsody" in white tie and tails while a chorus line of girls from the Cotton Club School of the Dance trucked and jived. Gertrude Michael, a specialist in bitches, crooned a hymn to "sweet marijuana," at the end of which she was mown down by a machine gun wielded by Charles Middleton, later famous as Ming the Merciless, emperor of the universe, in the *Flash Gordon* serials. In another number, half-naked showgirls waved ostrich fans in a surprisingly effective imitation of surf while Kitty Carlisle, wearing a net body stocking with a few strategically placed fronds, "swam" to a desert island and a clinch with her German costar, Carl Brisson, whose plodding performance reflected his former career as a boxer.

For my audience at La Pérouse, I described only edited highlights of this experience, but it was enough to seize their attention. I used it to point out the features of the room where we were dining. Was it possible, I suggested, that the lithe, near-naked Kitty of 1934, frolicking in a Hollywood surf of ostrich plumes, came close to the kind of creature that La Pérouse expected to discover in the South Seas—the seductive siren who lured sailors to their doom?

"In *Murder at the Vanities*," I concluded, "the showgirls enter the theater through a stage door above which is the sign 'Through These Portals Pass the Most Beautiful Women in the World.'" Raising my glass, I went on, "All these years, I've wondered if this claim was true—and now, looking at our guest of honor, I see that it was."

As always with show business, nothing succeeded like excess. The group applauded. Kitty beamed. Patting the chair beside her, she said, "My dear, you must come and sit by me."

For the rest of the dinner, we exchanged showbiz gossip, of which she had an inexhaustible stock.

"The 'Sweet Marijuana' number in *Vanities*," I said. "You'd never get away with it now."

She leaned toward me conspiratorially. "Darling, you can't imagine how green I was. I'd never heard of the stuff, let alone smoked it. And those lyrics about 'put me to sleep, sweet marijuana'? Well, 'marijuana' sounded a little like 'marimba,' so I thought it was a Mexican musical instrument!"

As we broke up three hours later, she gave me a business card. "Next time you're in New York, please visit." She squeezed my arm. "Promise, now."

A year later, I did call on her in the vast apartment on Manhattan's East Side. She'd just returned from another performance of her one-woman show and looked tired, but still found the energy to lead me along her gallery of paintings by famous songwriters: canvases of varying skill, executed by Jerome Kern, Noel Coward, and George Gershwin. I'm not sure she remembered much of that night at La Pérouse. Even my recollection was clouded. But a dinner had been the correct way to celebrate what would become her last visit to Paris: she died the following year, aged ninety-six. The ritual, the ceremony, the sense of a sacrifice were all as should have been. As Arthur Miller said in *Death of a Salesman*, to such a person, attention must finally be paid.

18

Behind Closed Doors

I remember the first time I had sex. I kept the receipt.
GROUCHO MARX

L ike Maxim's across the river, La Pérouse was a
former brothel. In the 1890s its ground-floor lounge
was filled with chattering cocottes, either waiting for
a client to arrive or hoping to snare one. The upper
floors are still divided into *chambres séparées*: private
dining rooms, reached by narrow, winding staircases,
discreetly dark. Some, like the one where we ate, seat
twenty; others accommodate only two people, or three
at a pinch, on couches upholstered in red velvet.

What one did at home in sight of gossiping servants
risked becoming common knowledge, but what took
place in *chambres séparées* stayed there. Behind their
closed doors, everything was permitted. By the end
of the century, their mythology was sufficiently well

Maurice Chevalier with Maxim girls in the 1934 film of
The Merry Widow

known to inspire the aria *Komm mit mir ins chambre séparée*, which made an international hit of the 1898 Viennese operetta *The Opera Ball*. Maxim's in particular was so notorious for its private rooms and *poules de luxe* that the writers adapting Franz Lehár's operetta *The Merry Widow* into English moved the entire third act to Paris. The hero Danilo blows off his consular duties to enjoy a wild night, celebrating the prospect in "I'm Off to Chez Maxim."

> *At Maxim's once again*
> *I swim in pink champagne.*

When people ask what bliss is
I simply tell them, "This is."
Lolo, Dodo, Jou-jou,
Clo-clo, Margot, Frou-frou—
And when it comes to kisses,
Goodbye, my fatherland!

Before and after performances at the Paris Opéra, fashionable couples mingled in private rooms at the Hôtel Grand, just opposite Garnier's wedding cake of an opera house. Military officers, socialites, and politicians took off the edge by injecting the day's fashionable drug, morphine. Those not into dope could enjoy the attentions of *grandes horizontales*, as expensive courtesans were known. Émile Zola, well acquainted with vice, described his archetypal cocotte Nana meeting clients in the Grand, and later dying in one of its rooms.

At Maxim's, La Pérouse, and the Grand, discretion counted for more than the cuisine. If a guest requested music to smooth a seduction, a trio or quartet would be hidden behind screens or a pianist hired to play *en sourdine*, out of sight behind a curtain. For even greater intimacy, one could have a violinist blindfolded if necessary—playing right there in the room. (On one occasion, the best Gypsy violinist in Vienna was imported for the evening to gratify a guest nostalgic for the days of the Hohenzollerns.) Should a gentleman's companion for the evening stand him up or prove unsatisfactory, replacements were available in the bar. Known as *plats du jour*—daily specials—these women loitered over a glass of champagne until the head waiter came to the door, singled out the girl closest to the client's taste, and signaled by a touch of his forefinger to a mole on his cheek that she was required upstairs.

In such places, crowned heads and celebrities could enjoy intimate dinners and the most piquant of desserts, confident of being neither discovered nor disturbed. If the unthinkable should happen, however, a tunnel was rumored to lead from La Pérouse through the caves via the former Convent des Augustins to the security of the Senate.

The maitre d', sommelier, and *fonctionnaire* in charge of greeting each arrival were almost as important as the chef de cuisine. They remain so today. Many American restaurants retain a sleek young woman with no task more demanding than keeping track of reservations. Her equivalent in Paris is very different. Older and male, he can recognize by sight the nation's four or five hundred most famous faces, and knows not only the correct forms of address for a count, a Saudi prince, a cardinal, and a judge, but the order of seniority in which they should be accommodated.

Above all, restaurants of the first rank guarantee discretion—not simply about the identity of clients and their companions, but also what they eat. On occasion, such information has had political significance. As the revolutionaries of 1968 mellowed into run-of-the-mill politicians and began to live well, the press, having checked up at their preferred restaurants, attacked them for their diet, labeling them contemptuously *gauche caviar*—caviar socialists.

When Édouard Balladur ran against Jacques Chirac for the presidency in 1995, the restaurant where both ate lunch leaked the information of what they ordered. M. Balladur, who looked like a throwback to the eighteenth century, more comfortable in a powdered wig, favored herrings in olive oil, while M. Chirac, a tough, practical politician in the mold of Lyndon Johnson, went for *tête de veau*, a robust country dish made of meat from a calf's head embedded in jelly. Once word got around, diners were invited to order the dish preferred by their candidate. Most chose *tête de veau*, so nobody was surprised that Balladur fared catastrophically in the first round of the election, with a mere 18.6 percent of the vote. Chirac won the runoff at a walk.

A few months before the dinner at La Pérouse, I'd experienced traditional Parisian restaurant diplomacy at work just a short walk along the Seine. It was our first visit to another of Paris's culinary institutions, the Michelin-starred Tour d'Argent. Although the restaurant itself is on the sixth floor, with spectacular views over the Seine, particularly at night, one enters at ground level. After one staff member confirms your reservation, another directs you to the elevator, a third ushers you into it, while others wait six floors above to welcome you and conduct you to your table.

We arrived in the lobby at the same time as a French couple who, from the effusive greetings of the staff, were regulars. While one man checked our credentials, another conducted the newcomers straight to the elevator, where we joined them a few moments later.

At the top, the door opened on the smiling face and impeccable black suit of yet another host. He faced a tricky situation. At the rear of the car were two old and valued clients. Facing him, however, were three strangers who, for all he knew, might be rich enough to buy the building and everyone in it.

The ballet of deference that followed would have done credit to Versailles under Louis XIV. His smile to the couple behind us was modified by a glance toward us and a barely raised eyebrow, as if to say, "My apologies—but you see how it is; duty demands . . ." At the same time, without quite separating our threesome he ushered the couple from the rear of the elevator, shook the man's hand, kissed that of his wife, then handed them off to another flunkey before turning to us with a look that said, "And now, my dear new friends . . ." After such a welcome, the panorama of nighttime Paris and the four-hundred-page wine list were almost anticlimactic.

· 19 ·

Love and Fresh Water

*And in that poverty, and in that quarter across the street
from a Boucherie Chevaline and a wine-cooperative,
he had written the start of all he was to do. There never
was another part of Paris that he loved like that, the
sprawling trees, the old white plastered houses painted
brown below, the long green of the autobus in that round
square, the purple flower dye upon the paving, the sud-
den drop down the hill of the rue Cardinal Lemoine to
the River, and the other way the narrow crowded world
of the rue Mouffetard.*

ERNEST HEMINGWAY, "The Snows of
Kilimanjaro"

n Michael Powell's quietly insightful film *I Know
Where I'm Going*, a London millionaire and his fiancée, played by Wendy Hiller, confound the people
of the outer Hebrides with their readiness to throw

money around. The locals build them a swimming pool and sell them salmon but shake their heads as they do so, wondering why they don't swim in the sea and catch their own salmon in waters that teem with them.

When Hiller proffers a pound note to pay for a telephone call, the lady in the post office recoils from it as from a snake.

"She wouldn't see a pound note from one pension's day to another," explains her friend, Roger Livesey, as he doles out a few coins.

"People around here are very poor, I suppose," says Hiller.

"Not poor, they just haven't got any money."

"I've been rich and I've been poor," says gang girl Gloria Grahame in Fritz Lang's *The Big Heat*. "Believe me, rich is better."

I'll have to take her word for it, since I've never been rich. I've had money, but that's not the same thing. Early in life, I realized that the size of one's bank balance was no measure of wealth. Moving to France simply confirmed it.

The Scots and the French share a greater respect for family, tradition, and national heritage than for fortune. Maybe that explains France's long-standing affection for Scotland. Napoleon dismissed the English as "a nation of shopkeepers," but the French have always regarded the Scots as fallen kings and queens, proud, warlike, and deeply respectful of family ties—in short, just like them. Why else would the French shelter two pretenders to the British throne, Mary, Queen of Scots, and Charles Stuart, alias Bonnie Prince Charlie? That both attempts ended in disaster only increased their respect. A nation that reveres Napoleon develops a connoisseur's appreciation of failure.

One summer in the 1970s, I was besotted with a girl who lived in a one-room studio on Place de la Contrescarpe, at the head of rue Mouffetard. We made love on a mattress on the bare board floor to the music of the accordion player who busked for coins in the cafés two floors below, and with no money to eat out, we subsisted, as the French say, "on love and fresh water."

Sitting by the window, enjoying the day's first coffee while my love slept, I mentally cataloged the morning sounds; the tinny chime of the bells from Église Saint-Médard, the clink of crates of wine being delivered to the cafés, the rumble of beer kegs rolled across cobbles, the splash of water sloshing down the gutters, the scratch of the street sweepers' brooms as they brushed cigarette butts and other debris out of the stream, to be swept up later.

Any local seeing my look of contentment would

have dismissed me as a romantic fool. Real poverty was never glamorous. Rue Mouffetard used to have one of the worst reputations in Paris. "Mouffetard" derives from *mouffle*—old French for "stink." The river Bièvre, which once ran at the bottom of the hill, served tripe butchers and tanners of leather until the stench of hides and the dog shit used to remove hair became so stifling that it was paved over. The smell disappeared but the name stuck.

To both Honoré de Balzac and Victor Hugo, Mouffetard signified misery. Balzac's *Le Père Goriot* takes place mostly in one of the residential tenements, "in a vale of crumbling stucco, watered by streams of black mud." In Hugo's *Les Misérables*, the fugitive Jean Valjean is so moved by the poverty of other panhandlers around Saint-Médard that he gives them money. Hearing of a beggar who presses coins on other beggars, his nemesis, the detective Javert, stakes out the church, sending the hapless Valjean once again on the run. Let nobody say a good deed goes unpunished.

In the 1730s, the church became famous as the home of a curious sect, the convulsionists. People praying at the grave of François de Pâris, a pious deacon, claimed miraculous cures. But some were seized by convulsions. Like Holy Rollers in the American South, they sang, danced, spoke in tongues, stamped on bibles, barked

The convulsionaries of Saint-Médard

like dogs, and swallowed glass or hot coals. Alarmed, Louis XV ordered the church closed, inspiring a protester to post this notice:

By order of the King
It is forbidden to the Divinity
To perform any more miracles
In this vicinity.

The convulsionists moved elsewhere, but a hint of the sect survives. On Sunday mornings, people still gather at the foot of rue Mouffetard to dance and sing in the street.

That Ernest Hemingway, James Joyce, and George Orwell once lived a few streets away gave a delicious frisson to the square, on my side at least. Their Contrescarpe, however, had been a meaner place. Back then, "honey carts" still arrived in the early hours to pump out the cesspools, a feature of the Paris night that Brassaï also recorded. He captured the silhouettes of the sanitary workers and the steam rising against the light of the street lamps. The stink that went with it fortunately didn't photograph.

In Hemingway's time, the establishment across the square, now decidedly up-market, had been the Café des Amateurs,

> *a sad, evilly run café where the drunkards of the quarter crowded together and I kept away from it because of the smell of dirty bodies and the sour smell of drunkenness. The men and women who frequented the Amateurs stayed drunk all of the time, or all of the time they could afford it, mostly on wine which they bought by the half-liter or liter.*

In 1929, George Orwell lived nearby, on rue du Pot-de-Fer, and worked as a *plongeur*—a dishwasher—in the hotels and restaurants of the right bank. He had nothing good to say about the area. Half a century later, not much had changed. In his spy novel *Smiley's People*, John le Carré dismissed it as "a quartier once celebrated for its large population of the poorer Russian émigrés" and froze it in a frigid amber of ennui. "The street was grey and narrow, and shuttered, with a couple of small *hotels de passe* and a lot of cats. It was a place, for some reason, of peculiar quiet."

Contrescarpe deserves better—not for its achievements, which are negligible, but its deficiencies, which are multitudinous. Failure suffuses the area as pervasively as the smell of drains. In the early 1930s, Jacques Deval chose Contrescarpe as the setting for his play *Tovaritch*. Mikail and Tatiana, a Russian prince and princess, have fled to Paris with the imperial crown jewels, placed in their care by the royal family before their assassination. Although their Russia no longer exists, the couple continue to guard the gems, refusing to sell them. Instead, they live in poverty, begging and shoplifting until they take jobs as butler and maid for a bourgeois family whose members they civilize, educate, and inspire by example.

An international stage hit in 1933, *Tovaritch* was popular even in Berlin, where Hitler, after assuring himself that Deval was not Jewish, saw it three times. It was filmed twice, first in France in 1935. Studying the film when it was rediscovered in the early twenty-first century, scholars realized, in a scene where Iréne Zilahy as Tatiana tries to steal artichokes from a market, that the extra stepping out of a nearby building was none other than Louis-Ferdinand Céline, author of the classic realist novel *Voyage to the End of the Night*. In the Depression, even great writers took work where they could get it.

For the second film, made in Hollywood, Broadway veteran Robert E. Sherwood rewrote Deval to soften his lesson—that hard times call for stern measures. Though Charles Boyer and Claudette Colbert are suspiciously well-fed for starving aristos, they still upstage their employers with effortless style. At the conclusion, however, reality intrudes, as in the original. The commissar who once tortured them and raped Tatiana comes to Paris to negotiate a deal for Russian oil. When he explains that the imperial fortune would save Soviet Russia from having to sell out to French, British, and American interests, Mikail hands it over.

His shrugging acceptance of defeat marks *Tovaritch* as indisputably a Moufftard play. Nothing symbolizes this more acutely than the public swimming pool on rue Thouin, just behind Contrescarpe. It's named for the

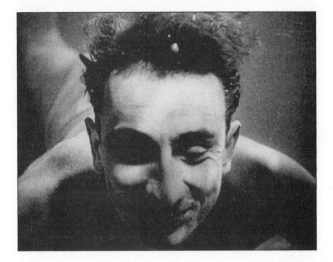

Jean Taris

now-forgotten swimming champion Jean Taris. Though he held a number of French records, Taris was a stroke too slow for the foreign competition. At the 1928 Olympics in Amsterdam, he lost to Larry "Buster" Crabbe, who went on to Hollywood, playing Flash Gordon and Buck Rogers.

Had Taris been more of a bruiser, he, and not Crabbe, might have had the film career. There is even a short documentary about him, made by one of the finest directors of the time, Jean Vigo. It shows him clowning around a pool, swimming underwater, and displaying his speed in a race. After that, however, both Vigo and Taris appear to lose interest. The film ends ruefully. Taris stoically puts on a long overcoat, raises his bowler hat, picks up his suitcase, and disappears into history. The Piscine Jean Taris is meant as his monument, but his name means nothing to the people who swim there. This is no place for stars.

Part Two

NIGHT 2:
TASTE

❈ ·20· ❈

Poor Food?

It's terrible
the faint sound of a hard-boiled egg firmly cracked
on a tin counter
it's terrible this faint sound
when it stirs the memory of a starving man.

JACQUES PRÉVERT, "La Grasse Matinée"

(Sleeping In)

Forty years ago, the Greek island of Hydra was just a backwater at the end of a four-hour boat ride from Athens. The little *kafeneion* where I went looking for lunch wasn't the most appealing, just the only one still open after the departure of the ferry. How was I—a young Australian, visiting Europe for the first time—to know that the moment the tourists disappeared on the boat that brought them, so would all the cafés and bars as the locals closed up shop and went home to eat or sleep?

Back then, Greek restaurants still honored the tradition of "the look"—a visit to the kitchen to check what was on offer. But in this case the cook, a gaunt woman in an apron with enough stains to feed a family for a week, appeared diffident, particularly when I showed interest in a vegetable stew simmering at the back of the stove.

Tugging my sleeve, she drew me to the back door. Just outside, a scrawny sheep revolved on a spit over palely glimmering coals.

"Lamb," she said encouragingly. "Is good."

I shook my head and pointed to the stew: "This."

"No, no. Zis . . . zis is . . ." She groped for the words. "Poor food."

She didn't mean it was bad, but rather that it was what the locals ate. Unlike tourists, they couldn't afford to dine every day on lamb.

Grudgingly, she served me a plate of what I'd come to know as *briami* but which Greeks call simply *tourlou*—"mix-up": zucchini, eggplant, onion, potatoes, and tomatoes, all richly oiled, herbed, and garlicked, then braised with a little water. With a basket of fresh pita to mop up the sauce and a carafe of the local red *demestica*, I couldn't have asked for a better meal. My appreciation won her over, since she plonked down a battered pot of fragrant sweetened coffee and homemade baklava oozing honey and waved away my payment. Briefly, I had become one of them, the eaters of "poor food."

This was the culinary world in which I had been raised in rural Australia. For people like my parents, who'd endured the Depression and World War II, meat was a luxury reserved for Sundays, when a chicken or a leg of lamb provided the week's biggest meal. The French movie star Jean Gabin, who began his career in the 1920s, was asked why he became an actor. "So I could eat meat every day," he shrugged. Meat every *day*? To most people of his generation—and that included my parents—this was inconceivable, even a little obscene.

We lived at the edge of town in a clapboard bungalow roofed in corrugated iron. On the acre of ground behind the house, we grew tomatoes and lettuce in summer, carrots and potatoes in winter. A dozen fruit trees, ancient and gnarled, provided tart apples for pies and bitter, thick-skinned oranges for marmalade. Our kitchen stove burned wood or, if we were lucky, coal, which my young brother and I scavenged from the railway embankment at the foot of our street. There was no snobbery about eating what we grew. It was how we survived.

At fifteen, I took a job with the railways that had furnished all that free coal and fled to the city. As a bachelor with little money, I taught myself to cook. Instead of taking women to restaurants, I invited them to my tiny apartment for dinners of asparagus with Hollandaise sauce or lamb roasted with fresh rosemary. What impressed them was the fact that in a country where, traditionally, men only entered the kitchen in search of a corkscrew, this one had cooked for them.

Once I settled in the United States, the concept of "poor food" became increasingly remote. I never expected to see it in Georgetown, the most prosperous neighborhood of Washington, D.C., and least of all in the home of a former high government official. My girlfriend was good friends with his daughter, who explained he'd lost his job in the last change of administration. The family had kept its silver and porcelain, but times were so hard they were surviving on food stamps. Nothing, however, would force them to lower their standards, least of all for their traditional Christmas dinner for more than twenty friends and neighbors, including my girlfriend and me.

Only someone raised in similar circumstances would have noticed the stratagems used by our hostess to create a—superficially, at least—lavish meal. Her decanters were Baccarat but I recognized the wine as supermarket burgundy. The well-flavored aspic of the jellied starter disguised the fact that the meat was stewed pork cheeks, while the host carved the rolled, stuffed lamb shoulder with such ceremony that one didn't notice the thinness of the slices and how liberally he piled each plate with baked potatoes, canned tomato casserole with cheese and breadcrumbs, creamed-corn pudding, and that southern specialty, Mock Oyster, in which eggplant baked with eggs and Ritz crackers miraculously assumes the flavor and texture of an oyster casserole.

I thought again of the cook on Hydra. Why should we be ashamed of using modest resources with intelligence and creativity? "Poor food" shouldn't be an apology, but a boast.

And then I moved to Paris.

As a working journalist since college, my new wife had never learned to cook. She loved to eat, however, particularly the dishes of her childhood as their housekeeper had prepared them.

"*Pot-au-feu*," she rhapsodized. "*Gratin d'endives au jambon. Hachis parmentier. Blanquette de veau . . .*"

Pot-au-feu? But that was just cheap cuts of beef simmered with potatoes, leeks, and turnips. *Hachis parmentier* was that old meat-stretching standby, Shepherd's Pie—minced leftover lamb baked under a layer of mashed potato. For *blanquette de veau*, one stewed tough cuts of veal, then cloaked them in the stock thickened with egg yolk. As for endive, few vegetables were cheaper, even if, as in the recipe she remembered, you rolled each one in ham and baked them in a cheese sauce.

Poor food!

Not to the French, however. To transform pig's blood into *boudin noir*, duck livers into *pâté*, and baked snails into *escargots*, a delicious dish that has become a national icon, wasn't economy but art.

Strictly from Hunger

*Do not devour with your eyes the dishes
brought to the table.*

   Christian Politeness, a manual of good behavior for
   Catholic schoolchildren

With its history of deprivation, Contrescarpe looks to be an unpromising place to explore a sense of taste—except that rue Mouffetard hosts one of the busiest food markets in Paris, a torrent of fruit, meat, cheese, fish, and wine spilling down the narrow street. To hungry men and women, its richness can overwhelm the senses. One author saw the produce as a painter's palette. "Colors of the four seasons on rue Mouffetard at midday. Cherry red, lemon yellow, orange orange, apple green, and radish pink." The English writer Michael Palin sounded almost delirious as he surveyed this cornucopia of edibles: "the smells of fresh-baked bread, cheese, coffee, crêpes, roasting chicken, almonds, herbs, sausages, shellfish and everything the French find so important in life induce a series of small olfactory orgasms."

While a demonstration of plenty makes more poignant the hunger of those who live here, a background of appetite expands one's appreciation of food. Balzac in *Le Père Goriot* chose a metaphor of eating to introduce his story of old Goriot and his enslavement to his greedy daughters. "Now and again," he wrote, "there are tragedies so awful and so grand that the impression they give is like a luscious fruit, soon consumed." Culinary images pepper the book. Of the greedy widowed landlady, Mme. Vauquer, he says, "her heart, like a larded partridge, sweltered before the fire of a burning desire to shake off the shroud of Vauquer and rise again as Goriot."

Hemingway, walking from his apartment on rue du Cardinal Lemoine to visit Gertrude Stein, detoured through the Luxembourg Gardens because it had no restaurants to distract him with savory aromas. He believed that modest hunger sharpened the other senses, increasing his appreciation of Cézanne's canvases in the Musée du Luxembourg. Back in his room, he snacked on clementines and roasted chestnuts bought from a street vendor—a supper as sparse as his prose.

For some, hunger encourages creativity; for others, it stifles it. Deprivation fed the inspiration of Norwegian novelist Knut Hamsun. In his autobiographical novel *Hunger*, he described waking hungry at five in the morning.

I wanted to go back to sleep but could not. I was wide awake and a host of thoughts flooded through my mind. Suddenly a few choice fragments came to mind, perfectly suitable for use in a rough draft, or to be serialized. Instantly I found, quite by chance, lovely phrases such as I had never conceived. I repeated them to myself slowly, word by word; they were excellent. And still more followed. I rose and snatched a pencil and paper from the table behind my bed. It was as though an artery had burst inside me, one word followed another, found its correct position, adapted itself to the context, scene piled on scene, events unfolded, one vessel after another bubbled in my mind, and I was enjoying myself immensely.

George Orwell's experience was exactly the opposite. Forced to starve for three days during his darkest days as a *plongeur*, he spent them in his rented room, re-reading the Sherlock Holmes stories.

*It was all that I felt equal to, without food. Hunger
reduces one to an utterly spineless, brainless
condition, more like the after-effects of influenza than
anything else. It is as though one had been turned
into a jellyfish, or as though all one's blood had
been pumped out and lukewarm water substituted.
Complete inertia is my chief memory of hunger.*

It's said that sex is the poor man's opera. In that case, eating is his folk music. And like folk music, the best is often found in the least pretentious places. True, there are establishments around Contrescarpe where haute cuisine flourishes. They include the Michelin-starred La Truffière. Sited in a seventeenth-century mansion, it offers truffles in almost every dish, with the option of even more on the side. One of its specialties elevates that nursery favorite, a boiled egg with toast fingers, to new heights. I can unreservedly recommend its *oeuf cuit à basse température, croquant de pain au jus, purée d'oseille, anguille fumée et truffe de Bourgogne, poudre de cèpes et échalotes avec la truffe blanche d'Alba* (soft-boiled egg, crisp bread with juice, sorrel purée, smoked eel and Burgundy truffle, cepes and shallot powder with white truffles from Alba). A unique culinary experience, and a mere $150 a plate.

But restaurants like La Truffière are in the minority. Those that don't serve ethnic food—Chinese, Greek, couscous, the ubiquitous pizza—rely on such staples of low-priced eating as the *salade composée* and the *tartine*.

The visitor who, scanning a bistro menu, says, "Oh, I'm not very hungry. I'll just have a salad" is seldom prepared for the *salade composée*. The food writer who described it as "cheese and meat decorated with a few pieces of lettuce" wasn't far wrong. While it resembles such American "dinner salads" as the Waldorf, the Cobb, and that gluey staple of Californian stand-up suppers, the peanut-sauced Chinese chicken salad, French eaters would protest at those dishes' stingy portions and lack of variety. The *composée* is a hungry man's salad, robust enough to see one through a long afternoon on the business end of a shovel. It's customarily served in a dish, not on a plate, and a deep dish at that, with ingredients heaped above the lip. Since *composée* means, literally, "compounded," it strives to include the maximum number of ingredients. A few will be greens—lettuce, mignonette, frisée, romaine, sometimes young spinach leaves, endive, watercress or mâche (Britain's lamb's lettuce)—but these exist mainly as spacing for the protein that makes this dish a meal.

Of these, hard-boiled eggs are standard. Expect at

least one, quartered. Cheese too: cubes of cantal, mozzarella, and chèvre. Lardons of salt pork, kernels of corn, cold boiled green beans and potatoes, perhaps artichoke hearts or hearts of palm. Croutons add body and crunch, usually in small dice, commercially produced, but occasionally replaced by squares of old bread, fried crisp in bacon fat or butter. Seldom included are onion or garlic, obnoxious if breathed around the office. Too creamy a dressing can reduce the salad to sludge, so most cooks stick to a simple vinaigrette, although occasionally one chances something richer and whisks a raw egg yolk into the oil, vinegar, mustard, honey, and salt.

After that, each cook uses his imagination. One of the most popular salads, *Niçoise*, in the style of Nice, on the Côte d'Azur, mixes tomatoes, hard-boiled eggs, anchovy fillets, tuna, olives, and capers. *Salade à l'italienne* uses the chewier varieties of pasta: spirali or farfalle. Dice of cooked beet, potato, and carrot make a *salade russe*. Other international variations include *salade norvégienne* (smoked salmon, capers), North African (couscous or tabouli), Greek (feta cheese, black olives, and slivers of salt-preserved lemons) and Mexican (red capsicum and shreds of corn tortilla).

From there, one moves into the terra incognita of *salades gourmandes*—salads for gluttons. For these, among cheeses, only Roquefort will do. Thin slices of smoked duck breast replace the workaday lardons, or, in the greediest variation, cubes of *foie gras*. This is where the less adventurous tourist gives up. I once watched an English tourist sort through a *salade gourmande*, fastidiously picking out the morsels of *foie gras* and placing them on the side of her plate. When she'd finished, she forked up a mouthful of greens and said brightly, "It's really quite good— once you get rid of the nasty bits."

$$ ❋ \cdot 22 \cdot ❋ $$

Proposing a Toast

ROD: *Um, I was gonna ask you who you think would win in a fight between a grilled cheese sandwich and a taco.*

DENISE: *Well, I think the grilled cheese sandwich—in a fair fight. But if it was prison rules, I'd put my money on the taco.*

Hot Rod, script by PAM BRADY

I n lunchtime popularity among cost-conscious eaters, the *salade composée* is rivaled only by the *tartine*.

Neither "on toast" nor "open sandwich" conveys the complexity behind the word. As a verb, *tartiner* means simply "to spread," while a *tartine* is the material, generally bread or a cracker, on which something is spread (*écrit des tartines* means "to write at great length"—like spreading butter too thickly on toast).

Simple in theory, the *tartine* encompasses everything

from Nutella on toast to a Bayonne ham and goat cheese *croquante basque*. A *tartine* in its most basic form, a length of baguette with butter and *confiture* or honey, is the preferred after-school snack of every French child. (A chain of stores for children's clothes is called Tartine et Chocolat.) Because of this, the French reach adulthood with a readiness to munch on any slice of bread with a toothsome topping. Of the 1.3 million sandwiches consumed in France each year, 62 percent are still the classic *jambon beurre*—ham on a buttered baguette—but exotic variations are creeping in. There is even an annual two-day sandwich-and-snack trade show to demonstrate that the *tartine*, like pizza, is now the plaything of chefs, something on which to show off their virtuosity.

One of the most popular food programs on French TV is *Le Meilleure Boulangerie de France*, a search for the nation's best baker. Two judges, dressed in white coats like orthodontists, travel to regional bakeries, nibbling slices of local loaves and watching every stage of their manufacture, from the mixing of the flour, water, salt, and yeast—the baguette contains no fat—to the kneading, leavening, and baking. Under French law, all these must take place on the baker's premises. It's literally illegal to freeze the dough as bakers do in other countries.

The next day, they review a selection of the baker's

products, smiling benignly at the wives and children who've put on their Sunday best and had their hair done for the occasion. After this, the judges are filmed strolling through some bucolic beauty spot—woods are popular, though they've browsed some medieval ruins—while they discuss the bread's quality in terms that would flatter a new selection of aphorisms by Lacan or a particularly searching reexamination of Alain Robbe-Grillet. Quotes from La Rochefoucauld and Voltaire fall like autumn leaves.

But bread deserves no less. To the French, it has an almost mystical significance. References to bread are scattered through French idiom. Of a person who began promisingly but fell on hard times, they say "He ate his white bread first"—dark rye bread being a sign of poverty. Speaking of his friend Luis Buñuel, Jean-Claude Carrière, who scripted his films and ghosted his memoirs, told me seriously, "He was good—like good bread." The phrase "our daily bread" carries religious significance. Marie-Dominique's grandparents still cut a cross in the underside of each loaf to acknowledge bread as the gift of God. If I carelessly place a baguette on the table flat side uppermost, she will automatically turn it round side up; to show it upside down is as degrading as lifting a woman's skirt.

Bread is also political. Traditionally, revolutions took place when the harvest failed and there was no grain for bread. Such a shortage helped ignite the revolution of 1789. Angry citizens walked from Paris to Versailles to demand Louis release wheat from the royal granary. As they walked, they chanted, "We're going to see the baker and the baker's little boy." During World War I, both the French and British were incensed when the government ordered bakers to stretch scarce wheat by adding flour from such lesser grains as millet and barley. To do so was almost sacrilegious.

Bread and the dishes that use it are central to the French diet. The most popular non-baguette bread dish, and the one with the longest pedigree, is the *croque monsieur*—literally a "mister's munch." At its simplest, this is a grilled cheese sandwich. But implied in the verb *croquer* is a degree of relish. *Tu es à croquer* means "you look good enough to eat."

As Welsh rarebit, grilled cheese on toast is a commonplace of Anglo-Saxon fast food. According to legend, pub owners in Wales invented it to keep clients drinking when they might otherwise have left the bar in search of a restaurant. By melting scraps of leftover cheese with ale and pouring the mixture over a slab of bread, they made a quick cheap snack, with the added advantages that the salt in the cheese created a thirst while its fat lined the stomach, minimizing the effect of alcohol and encouraging more drinking.

So many boozers reeled home full of bread, cheese, and ale that the rarebit gained a reputation for causing nightmares if eaten last thing at night. At the end of the nineteenth century, American comic book artist Winsor McCay drew *The Dream of a Rarebit Fiend*, about a man who, after gorging on melted cheese and beer, has bizarre hallucinogenic dreams. His bed flies off into space, with him barely clinging on.

In the 1950s, Britain's drinks industry simplified the bread-and-cheese combination even further, and with the same motives. A slab of cheddar on a plate with bread, butter, and a vinegary chutney such as Branston pickle became a ploughman's lunch. Served at the bar with, naturally, more beer to wash it down, it was an instant success both with drinkers, who didn't risk burning their tongue or dripping cheese on their suits, and pub owners, since it required no cooking. Munching their bread and cheese in the belief that, like industrial laborers of another era, they were enjoying their rightful midday refreshment, almost nobody realized that their "ploughman's lunch" was dreamed up by ad men.

Though it irks them, most French chefs concede that

the Welsh probably did invent the *croque*, but agreement isn't unanimous. People in the mountainous French Savoie region argued that they've enjoyed melted cheese and bread for centuries, either as *fondue*—cubes of bread impaled on a skewer and dipped into a bubbling mixture of cheese and beer—or *raclette*, in which a slab of cheese is held close to a grill and the softened surface scraped off, to be eaten with slices of ham, cold boiled potatoes, and pickled gherkins.

Nevertheless, when the first official recognition of cheese on toast appears, in Auguste Escoffier's *Le Guide Culinaire* in 1903, the father of modern cooking accepts the traditional source and describes it as "Welsh rarebit." He gives two recipes. The first recommends a thick slice of *pain de mie*—soft "crumb bread," like an English sandwich loaf—which should be toasted, buttered, spread with Gloucester or Chester cheese, sprinkled with cayenne pepper, and grilled. The second recipe calls for cubes of cheese melted in pale ale with English mustard, then poured over toast. Rivals immediately competed to improve on Escoffier's recipe. They spiced up the cheese mixture with Worcestershire sauce or anchovy essence. Others made a béchamel sauce with flour, butter, and milk; added cheese and other seasonings; poured it over a ham sandwich; and browned it under the grill.

The ideal bread for a *tartine* didn't appear until Paris baker Lionel Poilane introduced his whole meal sourdough loaf in the 1970s. Tough, flexible but tasty, *pain Poilane* never wilted, no matter how gooey the topping piled on it. Advertisements (cunningly provided by Poilane himself) appeared in café windows. They showed a rustic loaf floating over a tranquil countryside, with a message urging clients to sample *le vrai tartine Poilane*.

These days, the *croque* is as common in France as the burger in the United States, and subject to even more variations. Leading these is the *croque madame*, a *croque monsieur* but *à cheval*. (This doesn't mean "made with horse meat" but indicates a fried egg placed on top of the sandwich, "on horseback.") After that, you can have it with tomato, *à la provençale*; *à l'auvergnate*, in the style of the mountainous region of the Auvergne, with *bleu d'Auvergne* or St. Nectaire cheese; *gagnet*, with Gouda cheese and andouille tripe sausage; *à la norvégienne*, with smoked salmon instead of ham; *bolognese*, with meat sauce; *señor*, with tomato, onion, and chili salsa; or Hawaiian style, with (shudder) a slice of pineapple. The oddest variation is the cheese naan, a miscegenation of French and Indian cuisine in which the dough for naan bread is molded around grated Gruyère and baked in the clay tandoori oven. Unknown in the subcontinent, it's one of the most popular of all side orders in France's growing roster of Indian restaurants.

Some branches of McDonald's even offer a croque McDo, about which the less said, the better. More grisly still is the creation chosen by *Esquire* as "the most life-changing grilled cheese." Sounding more life-threatening than life-changing, it's served with a side order of ranch dressing for dipping and consists of two slices of Texas toast, two fillets of chicken, two varieties of barbecue sauce, some slices of bacon—and, oh yes, cheese: mozzarella and cheddar, though you'd be excused for not seeing them. "It's still a grilled cheese," insists the proprietor of the café that makes this horror, which is like saying that a venison steak is still Bambi.

In France, snobbery has dogged the *croque monsieur*. Nouvelle cuisine, with its emphasis on isolating and emphasizing the essence of each ingredient, shunned cheese and bread equally. No variations on the *croque* appear on the menus of those chic eateries where the jeunesse dorée gather. Any cafés loyal to the cuisine of gratification tend to lie off the beaten track and identify themselves by the décor of an earlier and less opulent era.

Walking up rue Guynemer alongside the disciplined

perfection of the Luxembourg Gardens, I turned into rue de Fleurus, heading toward the onetime home of Gertrude Stein. A few minutes early for my appointment, I stopped for the first time at Café Fleurus, just a few doors from the intersection. Inside, I pulled up short. From the abstract mural of colored tiles behind the bar to the glass vitrines filled with pencils, cigarette lighters, and postcards, it was the very image of postwar Paris. Though the ban on smoking in public places had put an end to the fog of cigarette smoke that hung over such places and exiled to memorabilia stores those heavy triangular Ricard ashtrays, the ghosts of a million Gauloises lingered in the yellow tint of the high cream-painted ceiling above the ancient light fittings.

Two elderly men manned the bar. No casting director could have chosen better faces. Without even opening their mouths, they announced their citizenship in that lost world where Boris Vian might be sitting at the rear of the café, idly working on a first draft of *Le Déserteur*.

> *I'll just be a beggar*
> *On the roads of France*
> *And whether in Brittany*
> *Or down in Provence,*

To all I will say
"Refuse to obey.
Don't let them make you
Fight in the war."

I'd first heard Vian's song forty years ago, at a sold-out concert in Sydney, sung (in French) by Peter, Paul and Mary—who, it seemed, harbored a hint of subversion under their white-bread exterior. Did more than a handful of people in that audience realize the song preached draft-dodging? If so, they soon forgot it in the ebullience of *If I Had a Hammer*.

The waiter plonking down a menu interrupted my fantasies. *"Je vous écoute."*

"Une pression." Unable to hide my admiration, I said, "Monsieur, I compliment you. Your décor . . . pure 1960s!"

"Pas du tout, m'sieur," he said proudly. *"Cinquante-deux."*

Nineteen fifty-two? So when this was new, Paris was still under reconstruction, coming back to life after the battering of the war. That made it almost too early for Belmondo and Bardot. Who then? Gene Kelly, who made *An American in Paris* the year before? Or Yves Montand, and the young Simone Signoret?

"Et quelque chose à manger?"

Although I didn't feel hungry, I studied the short menu out of politeness. Something caught my eye.

"Croque Fleurus? C'est à dire quoi?"

"La specialité de la maison, m'sieur," he said. *"Jambon et Fourme d'Ambert."*

A *croque monsieur* made with Fourme d'Ambert, my favorite blue cheese, and one of the oldest in France! Not as fatty or as salty as Roquefort, but with a musty whiff of the caves and cellars of the mountainous Auvergne of central France.

"D'accord. Croque Fleurus."

Even before I tasted it, I knew the *croque*, washed down with cold beer from the tap, would not disappoint. Like everything else in Café Fleurus, it was, in a word by which the French set great store, *convenable*—appropriate. Belmondo, Bardot, Montand, Vian . . . they belonged to a continuity that stretched back to Baudelaire, Rimbaud, Villon, even to the lady of the Unicorn, dreaming in her flowered field.

Part Three

NIGHT 3:
TOUCH

23

A Walk on the Wild Side

My loves of long ago were girls of humble birth.
Margot the laundress and the seamstress Fanchon.
Not too noble (pardon my French),
They were, you might say, Graces with dirty faces,
Nymphs of the gutter, Venuses from the city gates.
You see, my Prince . . . one had the ladies of long ago
As and where one could.

GEORGE BRASSENS, "The Loves of Long Ago"

I n the fifteenth century, it was believed that the disease of scrofula, a swelling of the lymph nodes, could be cured if the sufferer was touched by the hand of a monarch. At public ceremonies, Henry IV of France ministered to as many as fifteen hundred victims at a time. Louis XV blessed two thousand, but he sometimes moved anonymously through the city at night, seeking out those afflicted by the disease which, because of this superstition, was known as King's Evil.

There is no district of Paris where that world of superstition and deception seems closer than the Marais. As my aunts used to say of wayward cousins, it is no better than it should be. Even more so today, nothing there is what it seems. Antique façades are preserved but their uses change, so that a nineteenth-century shop front announcing *Boulanger* or *Pharmacien* actually sells handbags. Old houses are knocked into "boutique" hotels. Their tiny rooms look out on courtyards which, for all their optimistic landscaping, are still recognizable as airshafts.

Repeatedly threatened with demolition, the seventeenth-century mansions and crooked streets of the Marais barely escaped the wrecking crews of Baron Haussmann in the 1860s. Jewish merchants who settled there were shrewd enough to leave it looking derelict. By retaining the original name, which means "marsh" or "swamp," and maintaining the houses and streets in unattractive dilapidation, they kept it a slumberous slum until after World War II.

Such postwar movies as Jean Cocteau's *Orphée* and Marcel Carné's *Les Portes de la Nuit* show the district as it was at the time of Sartre and Camus: rundown and crumbling, plaster chipped, doors and windows bricked up, walls splattered with posters. Le Corbusier would have flattened the whole thing, replacing it with concrete *unites d'habitation* neatly spaced in a park, like some high-rise memorial. Instead, an expanding young middle class in search of cheap accommodation surged in, pulling back the dusty curtains and dragging its treasures into the light.

There, however, its transformation ceased. Alarmed by Paris's runaway gentrification, the state stepped in with laws that severely limited renovations. André Malraux, de Gaulle's minister for culture, revived one of Haussmann's more obscure rules and required all buildings to steam-clean their façades every thirty years. By the time I came to France, the transformation was almost complete. The Marais was chic. So many guidebooks warn visitors not to miss this supposedly undiscovered corner of the city that one can barely move for pedestrians spilling off the narrow sidewalks. It's also the preferred address for Paris's gay culture. On weekends, streets are closed to any cars but those of locals, and mobs block the sidewalks outside such hookup spots as the L'Open or Cox.

All this has made the Marais, of all the districts in

central Paris, the one I most avoid. It shares something with London's Soho, New York's West Village, and the Royal Mile in Edinburgh; a place to take out-of-towners; one more sight, like the Eiffel Tower and the Arc de Triomphe. So I initially resisted when Louise mentioned she was going there to hunt *fripes*—vintage clothes.

"You don't find it a bit . . . well, *vieux jeu*?"

"Some of my favorite *jeux* are *vieux*," she said, and, in return for lunch, offered to show me a Marais more *branché*—switched on—than the one I knew.

"Looks the same to me," I grumbled as we bucked pedestrian traffic on rue du Renard, the unlovely street that runs along the back of the Pompidou Center, and marks the western border of the Marais.

"You think? See across the road?"

From a wall in tiny Place Igor-Stravinsky, a white face six stories high rolled its eyes at me and held a finger to enormous lips. Who put that there? I crossed to check. Another work by star wall painter Jean-François Perroy, aka Jef Aérosol, it's called, appropriately, *Chuuuttt!*—Shsssh!

Chuuuttt! was too new for the guidebooks. But guides have never meant much here. Hotspots shift by the month, and businesses are lucky to last a season.

Pausing at a hat shop, Louise tried on a gaudy cerise beret from a display spilling onto the pavement. The place was so new they still hadn't painted out the signage of the previous owner, a Proxi minimarket.

The Marais churns. It always has. Though shops with signs in Hebrew bolstered its image as the Jewish quarter of Paris, that was fading fast. Gay culture has displaced many old delis and cafés. Laundromats are now get-fit centers, offering steam rooms and "happy ending" massages. Every *maison de presse* displayed the beefcake covers of the gay glossy *Têtu*. Bookshops flaunted images of washboard stomachs and jutting jockstraps. The largest bookseller in the Marais is Les Mots à la Bouche—literally, "words in the mouth," a pun on *l'eau à la bouche*—mouthwatering—and the perfect encapsulation of the district's prevailing sense: appetite. This is the city that kisses. Perfumeries scented the air with fragrances as the young and beautiful, flawless as shop window mannequins, prowled the narrow sidewalks. Everywhere, people ate as they walked, licking their fingers, holding hands, acknowledging that here the sense of touch reigned supreme.

To many, these sticky fingers and fumbling hands clashed with the district's synagogues and museums commemorating the dead of Auschwitz, but they were in the minority. No stranger to diaspora, the Jews of the Marais are once again on the move. The closing of Joe Goldenberg's, oldest and most respected of the Marais's deli restaurants, marked the end of an era. Edmund White found it "wonderfully cozy with its steaming bowls of chicken soup and dumplings and its goulash and poppy seed cake, its strolling gypsy violinists and palm readers, its pair of lazy, over-fed dogs and its floor-to-ceiling paintings of rabbis in their prayer shawls or of near-Chagall blue pigs and flying musicians." Sufficiently rugged to survive a 1982 attack by Arab terrorists in which a number of people died, Goldenberg's suffered more insidious assaults from the Bureau de Santé on its standard of hygiene. These proved more lasting and, in time, fatal.

Though a handful of Jewish bakeries still survive along rue Sainte-Croix de la Bretonnerie and rue des Rosiers, fewer offer traditional challah and strudel. The clientele has migrated to the two branches of LegayChoc, whose big sellers are bread rolls and jam tarts shaped like hefty genitalia. And Louise smiled at a sign outside the confectionery Les Paris Gourmandes on rue des Archives.

"It says they sell *coucougnettes*."

"So?"

"It means 'testicles.' "

Inside the tiny shop, smelling of chocolate and vanilla, the *vendeuse*, straight-faced, explained that the fuzzy pink spheroids were a typical confection of the south, made from almond paste molded around chocolate. We left with a glassine bag filled with them, just the thing to pass around with coffee at the next dinner party.

Louise abandoned me for an hour to rummage in the melee of Free'P'Star, one of Paris's growing roster of fripperies and *dépôts-ventes*—secondhand clothing stores. A poster on its door advertised Décors de Bordels, an exhibition of brothel photos being held opposite the old premises of Le Chabanais, once Paris's most luxurious whorehouse. Tempting though this was, I decided to spend the time at the truly weird but utterly French Musée de la Chasse et de la Nature.

Supposedly devoted to hunting and nature, the museum celebrates animals through the joy of slaughtering them. Armories of antique firearms lead to entire menageries of mounted heads. Paintings on the same theme decorate the walls. An exhibit invites us to identify birds by their song, presumably as an aid to shooting the edible ones. Elsewhere, sliding drawers in a series of elegantly designed cabinets display clay impressions of spoor and other signs of animals in the wild. Need to know what wolf droppings look like? Seek no farther.

I rejoined a slightly disheveled but triumphant Louise, clutching bulging bags. Apparently hunting had been good.

"I suppose you want to go to the L'As du Fallafel," I said. (*L'As*, by the way, means "The Ace.")

"Why?"

"Well . . . it's supposed to be the best in Paris . . . written up in the *New York Times* . . ."

"Exactly. Look at it."

Modishness had fallen like a curse on this modest lunch counter. Scores of hungry clients queued in the chill. Others wandered about the street, trying to eat bulging pitas and not drip tahini sauce on their clothes. Its prosperity irritates the rival falafel restaurant opposite, the owners of which glare at the competition and hand out leaflets stressing the authenticity of their product.

"Where, then?"

She pointed down the block. "Chez Marianne. If you don't mind vegetarian."

I didn't. Not when it was an overflowing taster plate of Moroccan-style falafel, stuffed peppers, humus, eggplant caviar, tzatziki, tarama, and a surprising combination of artichoke heart with orange peel, all served by the actual Marianne, identifiable from her portrait, busty and beaming, on the cover of the menu.

And dessert? Just a coffee—and an inspiration from Louise. Dipping into her purse, she fished out the bag from Les Paris Gourmands. Of course—*coucougnettes*, the perfect Marais delicacy.

As I walked back home across the Seine, my fingers were still sticky with the delicacies I'd nibbled at Chez Marianne. Their tackiness resonated with the omnipresent sense of appetite that hung over the ancient lanes and shops. I imagined walking those narrow thoroughfares at night, fingers gliding over old stone, slick tile, metal, flesh. Thanks to my daughter, one of the fashion-conscious young, the door was now temptingly ajar. With the taste of *coucougnettes* still on my tongue, I wondered what other secrets of the Marais remained to be discovered. I was soon to find out.

24

Love at Night

Three matches, one by one in the night
The first to see your face
The second to see your eyes
The last to see your mouth
And the darkness to remind me of all this as I squeeze
you in my arms.

JACQUES PRÉVERT, "Paris at Night"

I couldn't believe what I was hearing," murmured Angelina Belladonna, leaning forward over her *café crème* and *tarte aux cerises.*

"Such as?"

We were sitting in Au Petit Versailles, on rue François Miron, a narrow thoroughfare that snakes along on the edge of the Marais, threading through ancient churches and buildings that had been old and leaning when François Villon reeled drunkenly among them, shouting, "We must know who we are. Get to know the monster that lives in your soul; dive deep and explore it."

The morning sun streaming through the window illuminated one of the prettiest cafés on the right bank, although its *belle époque* painted ceiling and frontage jarred with what Angelina was telling me about some surprising events that took place just a few doors from the little apartment they had just rented.

"They just stand there," she said, "in their fur coats and high heels, and you just *know* there's almost nothing on underneath. They have a cigarette in one hand and a cell phone in the other, and they say the most *extraordinary* things!"

"Well, of course," I said. "That's Le Pluriel."

Nothing distinguished rue François Miron except perhaps its antiquity, but one address at least was extremely well known. Nothing about the exterior of the seventeenth-century *hôtel particuliare* at No. 14 looked particularly remarkable. Its exposed beams and crooked windows gave no hint that it housed one of Paris's most popular *échangistes*, or sex clubs.

On its website you could watch videos of its three levels of cellars, where clients could enjoy a buffet supper, dance in the disco, drink at the bar, but also, more important, test the limits of what was possible between consenting adults. Ironically, one of the few acts forbidden in Le Pluriel was smoking. To light up, patrons had to climb to the street, where they used the opportunity to report to their friends on the night's activities. These were the ladies that so scandalized Angelina.

The following Sunday, around midnight, after dining with Angelina and her husband, we descended together to the ground floor and stepped out onto the sidewalk. A light rain was falling, sifting down through the streetlights and adding a sheen to the old stones.

"There they are," hissed Angelina.

About a dozen women pressed up against the façade to escape the rain. Most wore long coats, a few of them fur, but I spotted a Burberry, and one woman was tightly wrapped, Marlene Dietrich–like, in a belted garment of black leather that brought to mind horse whips and handcuffs. All wore heels so high that to walk more than a few meters would have invited a broken ankle. Not that any of them needed to. A phone call would bring a chauffeur or obliging husband from the parking station where they waited, napping or listening to late-night radio. Nothing among these people took place by chance. Sex was a serious business, to be approached with the care and formality of attendance at a vernissage on avenue de Marigny or a concert at Salle Pleyel. As one *partouzeuse* put it, "Does an orgasm deserve any less respect than a Chopin prelude or an etching by Matisse?"

As we passed, a few of the women turned away and lowered their voices, but most continued to murmur into their cell phones. I caught snatches of conversation in German, English, French. ". . . thought I was going to faint . . . *son bite . . . énorme, ma biche, je te jure . . .*"

That a streak of exhibitionism runs through this most formal of cultures isn't surprising. For most European intellectuals, writing, talking, or reading about sex has always been at least as entertaining as the act itself. The Hungarian playwright Ferenc Molnár, working on an operetta in the Budapest of the 1920s, was surprised, waiting one morning in the New York Café for his composer, to see him arrive with a suitcase.

"You know I've been trying for months to seduce the wife of the French ambassador," explained the musician.

"Of course," said Molnár "You talk of little else."

"Well, why not?" said the composer. "She's adorable. Anyway, I'm just a whisker off success, but now her wretched husband has been recalled to Paris. Naturally I must follow."

"Naturally," said Molnár. "And yet . . ." He lowered his voice. "My friend, which will give you greater pleasure: shtupping the lady or describing it to us in the café afterward?"

The composer didn't hesitate. "Well, of course, describing it."

Bending close to his ear, Molnár, said, "So why not tell us as if you had enjoyed the lady and save yourself the trip?"

The logic was incontrovertible. The composer stayed, the story was told, and the lady remained to be enjoyed another day.

Although Molnár was Hungarian, his was a particularly French solution—except in one detail. While Frenchmen frequently flaunt their conquests in conversation, it's women who put it on paper. When Jane Fonda lived with director Roger Vadim in the 1960s, the wall between their bedroom and bathroom was glass—a useful metaphor when dealing with France's female intellectuals, who have seldom been backward in spilling the conjugal beans. The men whose secrets they exposed didn't always agree. When Simone de Beauvoir described her affair with Nelson Algren, complete with quotes from their love letters, the author of *The Man with the Golden Arm* and *A Walk on the Wild Side* snarled, "Whores close the door, but Simone de Beauvoir leaves them wide open and invites the public and the press to come in."

Despite these protests, women continued to make the running. Emmanuelle Arsan's *Emmanuelle* and Pauline Réage's *Histoire d'O* inspired films, TV series, and numerous sequels. In the case of the sadomasochistic *Histoire d'O,* there are clubs in many countries that meet to explore the world it created. One can go on *Histoire d'O* holidays, even cruises. English actress Jane Birkin's relationship with singer Serge Gainsbourg is lavishly documented by her raunchy performances in the films he directed, such as *Je T'aime Moi Non Plus,* and in their quirky magazine appearances. For the Christmas 1974 issue of *Lui,* the French equivalent of *Playboy,* the couple showed off the latest from Valentino and Dior, posing for photos in which Serge, suavely dressed in velvet smoking jackets and silk suits, spanked and pulled the hair of Jane as a means of showing off her lingerie.

Anyone who delves into France's social and cultural history stumbles sooner or later on *la partouze,* as the French call group sex. It has a long history, particularly among the elite. The surrealists shared partners as a matter of course. Édouard Mesens, senior figure of the Brussels group, and his wife Sybil were enthusiastic *partouzeurs,* Mesens's bisexuality adding extra spice. Between 1927 and 1929, poet Paul Éluard and his wife Gala and Max Ernst lived in a semipermanent ménage à trois.

Orgy in the Bois de Boulogne, 1927

With hopes of adding handsome young Salvador Dalí to the mix, Éluard took Gala to Cadaqués in August 1929 to meet him. Instead of turning the trio into a quartet, Gala left Éluard to become Dalí's wife and muse.

Expatriates took up the practice with enthusiasm. As most of the references in Cole Porter's *Let's Do It* are plural—birds, bees, Lapps, Letts—it may be the *partouze* that he's celebrating. As an adoptive Parisian during the 1920s, he saw "the best upper sets" doing it, and participated enthusiastically.

On warm evenings, Harry and Caresse Crosby, wealthiest of the American exiles, sometimes led a convoy of Bugattis and Duesenbergs to the wooded park of the Bois de Boulogne, parked in a circle, facing inward, then stripped off to fondle and fornicate in the blaze of the headlights. The association of sex and the automobile survived well into the 1980s. It was common knowledge that, if you drove to Porte Dauphine, a roundabout on the main route west out of Paris, put on your turn indicator and cruised in the slow lane, other cars would link up until the first peeled off, leading the group to a suitable location for a *partouze*.

The custom remained technically under cover until the appearance in 2002 of a memoir called *La Vie Sexuelle de Catherine M*. In forensically precise prose, Madame M, actually Catherine Millet, detailed thirty years of semipublic fornication with a bewildering range of partners. The *partouze* about which she wrote was very much top person's sex. Scorning what she called "the carousel of Porte Dauphine," her group gathered in private clubs, apartments, and the walled gardens of rural châteaux. Which was not to say she didn't fancy the occasional change of space, sampling the pleasures of parking stations, workmen's huts, or the back rooms of bars frequented by truck drivers and cabbies. She also pleasured herself with her dentist and his nurse in the chair, and with moving men in their van as they shifted paintings from airport to art gallery, the driver watching in the rearview mirror. When not having sex in company, confessed Millet, she also enjoyed exposing her body naked in public and being photographed doing so.

These revelations would have attracted little attention from a housewife or secretary. But Millet is a respected art historian who edits the monthly *Art Press* and wrote the definitive guide to French contemporary painting. Critics inclined to dismiss her stories as erotic fantasies, like *Emmanuelle* and *Histoire d'O*, were startled when she produced photographs taken by her husband, novelist Jacques Henric. Though not into the *partouze* himself, Henric tagged along on some of her excursions and cataloged her public exposures. Stories of their adventures, as well as a selection of unconventional holiday snaps, appeared in his own book, *Légendes de Catherine M.*

Their trips included one to Portbou, on the French-Spanish border. It's where art historian Walter Benjamin, author of the important text *The Work of Art in the Age of Mechanical Reproduction*, committed suicide with his mistress in 1940 while fleeing the Nazis. After examining the hotel room in which Benjamin spent his last night, Henric

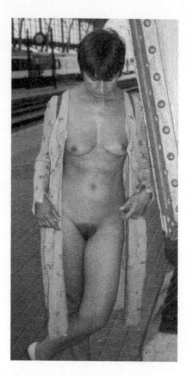

Catherine Millet at Portbou

photographed Millet seminaked in the cemetery where
he's buried. To complete the holiday, they visited Portbou
railway station, one of the busiest in Europe.

"Saturday fourteenth August 1999," wrote Henric
in breathless cinematic shorthand. "Le Talgo [express

train] heading for Barcelona passes through at high speed. Catherine is seated on a bench. The wind from the Talgo lifts the right panel of her dress. Her thigh is naked." More than the thigh, in fact—made clear as she stands up and walks toward the speeding train, dress unbuttoned from neck to hem. One can imagine the astonished passengers—"Did you just see . . . ?"

The *partouze* became front-page news again in 2012 when economist Dominique Strauss-Kahn, former minister in the French government, head of the International Monetary Fund, and possible candidate for president of the Republic, confessed to living a "libertine" life and participating in orgies all over Europe. Cleared of charges that he raped a hotel maid in New York, he was indicted in France for "aggravated pimping" over a sex party in a Madrid nightclub. Asked if any of the women at his parties were prostitutes, DSK, as he's known, responded that he had no way to tell, as, being naked, they carried no ID. You might detest the arrogance but you have to admire his style.

25

Skin-Deep

No mask like open truth to cover lies,
As to go naked is the best disguise.
William Congreve, *The Double Dealer*

'd known Sandy since my first days in France, when she ran a bookshop on the unfashionable fringes of Montparnasse. A native of Iowa, lean and genial, she was then married, though not happily, to a Frenchman who roamed the world, rifle in hand, intent, it seemed, on killing at least one of every species.

When the marriage collapsed, she sold the shop and disappeared into the American hinterland, never, I assumed, to be seen in Paris again. So it surprised me when we ran into one another at Bloom Where You Are Planted, one of those events where speakers and stall-holders hype quick fixes for the despair that afflicts many new arrivals in France.

"I was thinking of you!" she said. "You're just the man I need to help with a new project."

I flinched. Sandy's schemes were inevitably labor-intensive. For a while, she'd proposed holding a summer school at her country house, her husband's former hunting lodge. Students would hear lectures on impressionism or *Ulysses* in the morning but spend the afternoon blasting local wildlife in the surrounding forests. I pleaded deficient marksmanship and a horror of loud noises, and heard no more about it.

"If it's that summer school thing . . . ," I began.

"Oh, God, no!" She dismissed it with a wave of her hand. "This is quite different. And right up your street."

We wandered across the river into the Marais, where she kept a tiny apartment as a pied-à-terre, and took an outside table at Les Philosophes, one of the cafés along rue Vieille du Temple. Usually crowded with tourists eager for atmosphere, at this hour of the morning it was almost empty.

The streets, however, were full, not with tourists but with locals, out to do their marketing. I was reminded again of how, in these narrow streets, traditional limits of personal space broke down. Pedestrians passed so close that a skirt or coat tail might brush your back. Conversations became public property. Eyes met between tables, with mutual interest frankly expressed.

"This idea is absolutely perfect for you," Sandy began.

"Really?" Twenty years of listening to get-rich-quick projects had made me cynical. Remembering how Diaghilev responded to Jean Cocteau when he suggested a collaboration, I risked a quote from the great entrepreneur.

"Étonne-moi," I said. Astonish me.

She did.

"I'm going to make pornographic movies," she said. "And I want you to write them."

In Los Angeles, I knew people in the adult film business. A friend designed the "porn Oscars," known as the Heart-Ons, presented each Valentine's Day by the X-Rated Critics Organization. He smuggled a photographer friend and me into the award ceremony to see prizes handed out for Best Blow Job and Best Anal Intercourse. One recipient thanked "all the men who made it easy for me and all the women who made it hard for me." *Playboy* published my wondering account, although the editors discarded my title, "In the Playpen of the Damned," substituting "The Night of a Thousand Orifices."

"Why on earth would you want to make porn? There's miles of it in every DVD store. Even on regular TV."

"People of our age just don't identify with the kids in these movies. I think older audiences would be interested in seeing people more like themselves. Who would you rather watch—a couple of teenagers, or, say, Catherine Deneuve or Alain Delon?"

My instinctive response was "Neither." Instead I changed tack. "What sort of films are you thinking of?"

"Well, how about characters from history? Nobody seems to be doing that."

And with good reason. In the golden days when porn was shot on film rather than video, ambitious producers made versions of such period classics as *Bel Ami*, *Fanny Hill*, even the memoirs of Casanova. All failed because historical costumes and sets cost too much and audiences were just as happy with a contemporary story shot around a swimming pool in Topanga Canyon.

"Think of it!" Sandy said. "Héloïse and Abélard, Madame de Montespan, Marie Antoinette—and that's just France."

I stirred my coffee and, over her shoulder, watched the woman sitting behind us. If she tilted her chair back any further to eavesdrop, she risked toppling into the aisle.

"What about locations?"

She waved away this minor complication. "We can use my country place. There are dozens of rooms."

"But you've never made a movie."

"How hard can it be? The producers I've met are such dopes."

"But . . . do you have any idea what it would cost?"

"Not in detail. I thought you might help me with a whatchamacallit."

"Budget?"

"Yeah, budget."

Her confidence was unassailable. "Assuming you did manage to make the films, how would you distribute them?"

"I haven't got to that yet. Gotta make them first."

"What about performers?"

"Oh, I know some people. And there are these *échangiste* magazines—you know, for swingers. I thought I could advertise there. So . . . are you in?"

"Let me think about it."

But I didn't—not seriously.

Aside from period filming being notoriously expensive and time-consuming, I didn't fancy her chances of finding talent among the amateurs in the personals. And if she did manage to create the films, any pirate could copy a DVD and, by posting it on one of the numerous free porn Internet sites, wipe out all chance of profit. Rating her chances at slim to none, I pleaded pressure of work and bowed out. Which made the email she sent six months later all the more astonishing.

"Well, I did it!" said the message. "See attached."

The MP4 video ran for seven minutes. It began with a printed introduction in copperplate on a background that imitated parchment.

PAST PASSIONS PROUDLY PRESENTS
THE PRINCESS IS SERVED

The credits dissolved in on a candle-lit chamber, period indeterminate. As a husky man with a moustache embraced a lady in a robe of blue silk, a commentary, delivered in a breathlessly excited female voice, explained that she was Marguerite de Navarre, one of the sixteenth century's most accomplished sensualists, author of the erotic tales known as the *Heptaméron*. Her partner didn't need any introduction. Like most male performers in this kind of cinema, he was simply an all-purpose hunk: The Meat.

With a minimum of foreplay, the two lurched toward the bed, where Marguerite, wig now crookedly askew, opened the blue gown and lay back. Watching her companion hard at work, I thought of the old joke about the American girl, just back from Paris, praising her French lover's expertise.

"Where else would you find a man who licks your navel?" she asks.

"Why is that so great?" her friend says. "My boyfriend does that all the time."

Her companion raises an eyebrow. "From the inside?"

If Marguerite's body language could be believed, her lover was giving more than adequate satisfaction.

"*Mon amour, oh, mon amour,*" she moaned.

But that accent . . . ? Did I detect echoes of Sioux City and Keokuk? Looking more closely, I recognized the face under the heavy makeup and unfortunate wig.

Sandy's enthusiasm for middle-aged porn made sense at last. She had found a way to bloom where she was planted.

26

Crazy by Night

Sex is not romantic, particularly when it is commercial-
ized, but it does create an aroma, pungent and nostalgic,
which is far more glamorous and seductive than the most
brilliantly illuminated Great White Way.

Henry Miller, *Quiet Days in Clichy*

There are times when I've felt an affinity with Nick Carraway, the narrator of *The Great Gatsby*. Eager to be thought one of the beautiful people, he's condemned to be a watcher, a facilitator, and, in his darkest hour, a pimp, helping Gatsby arrange a doomed reunion with Daisy.

I'm no stranger to the role myself. I've been recruited as a "beard" when illicit lovers wanted to meet in a hotel lounge without arousing suspicion—and who, in their eagerness to get upstairs, left me to pay for some high-priced cocktails, only half drunk.

The Crazy Horse Saloon

In London during the 1970s, when censorship still strangled the cinema, banned movies could sometimes be shown at theaters registered as "film clubs." As a working critic, I had automatic membership, and occasionally friends asked me to take them as my guest. The number peaked with *Maîtresse*, a prowl through the underworld of French S&M, about which director Barbet Schroeder seemed to know more than was healthy.

Since I moved to Paris, a few men have quizzed me about the gay scene—"just for background color, you know, for the new novel." And women have solicited my help in dipping a toe—and more—into the *échangiste* scene and those clubs where clients arrive with one companion but leave with another.

This time, however, it was my turn to make the proposal. When my friend Milou wafted into town on one of her periodic visits, I asked, "Would you like to go to the Crazy Horse?"

Along with the Moulin Rouge and the Folies Bergère, the Crazy Horse Saloon strip club is one of Paris's most famous nighttime attractions. But was there any way it could be incorporated into a night walk? And to which of the senses would it appeal? As it wasn't a place one visited alone, and Marie-Dominique had no interest in accompanying me, I thought of Milou. Fortunately, she accepted immediately.

Tall, stately, with a penchant for little black dresses and sensational lingerie, Milou drifts around the edge of the arts. One month, she's doing PR for a boutique opera company that performs avant-garde one-acters in abandoned warehouses. Next, she pops up as au pair—governess to the family of an Italian baritone. A century ago, she could have been one of Maurice Dekobra's *madones des sleepings*, those suave women who haunted the wagons-lits of the *Train Bleu*, preying on the card sharps and their victims who played high-stakes bridge to fill the hours between Paris and Rome.

On her last visit to Paris, we'd seen a performance of Ravel's *L'Enfant et les Sortilèges* at Opéra Bastille, then had supper at La Fée Verte, the absinthe bar on rue de la Roquette. A visit to *le Crazy* wasn't quite in the same league, but a little slumming never hurt anyone.

During more than half a century, the Crazy has accumulated a mythology. Salvador Dalí and other distinguished artists designed numbers for his girls. Georges Balanchine visited regularly. In *What's New Pussycat* Woody Allen works there.

"I help the girls dress and undress," he says. "It's twenty francs a week."

"Not much," commiserates costar Peter O'Toole.

Woody shrugs. "It's all I can afford."

To promote the film, Allen participated in a photo shoot for *Playboy* called *What's Nude Pussycat*, in which he played touch football with the girls. As they were topless, Woody also removed his shirt, offering a rare view of the unremarkable Allen physique. The girls invited Woody backstage. "I spent about an hour and a half in there, chatting with them," he wrote to a friend. "The fact that I didn't understand a word of it didn't matter. I just nodded my head and smiled and went on looking."

Nothing about the Crazy Horse Saloon marks it as particularly out of the ordinary. Like avenue George V itself, a wide thoroughfare lined with expensive hotels, boutiques, and cafés, it looks, at first glance, quite staid . . .

Except, of course, for the doorman, who's dressed in the uniform of a member of the Royal Canadian Mounted Police.

Milou didn't blink, but as we descended the curving stairs into the below-ground cabaret area, she did raise an eyebrow.

"It's a long story . . . ," I began.

In 1951, Alain Bernardin, an enthusiast for American culture, decided that what Paris needed was a square-dance club. Leasing some wine cellars of Avenue George Cinq, he converted them into the Crazy Horse Saloon, complete with a floor wide enough for the most extravagant do-si-do and allemande left, and a real western bar where dancers could quench their thirst . . .

"Plus a Mountie on the door," Milou concluded.

"Exactly."

When the club flopped, Bernardin resourcefully turned it into a strip club. Its main attraction was his then-wife, Micheline Bernardini. A nude dancer at the

Casino de Paris, she'd been the first woman to model the bikini swimsuit after regular mannequins refused to appear in anything so shocking.

There's nothing cowboy about the modern Crazy Horse. A dimly lit terraced amphitheater under a low black ceiling, it seats customers on red plush couches in cubicles separated by barriers that provide a bare minimum of privacy.

Scheduled for nine thirty, the show didn't begin until after ten, when the last latecomers had been lured in and the final drinks order extracted. Only then did the curtain rise on the tiny stage.

For the next hour and a half, we watched in respectful silence as twelve dancers, interchangeable as Barbies in their unerotic near-nudity, posed, minced, lounged, writhed, and pouted. None displayed the slightest crease. No flab, no sweat, and no body hair, except for a neat black pubic triangle.

Aiming for a topical repertoire, the current choreographer, Philippe Decouflé, had introduced an element of social comment. More than twenty years ago, I attended one of his first works. Presented as part of the Festival of Saint-Denis, the most left wing of Paris's so-called Red Belt of satellite towns, it was staged in an abandoned boiler house.

He'd gone upmarket since then, while retaining his socialist bias. In one number, an anguished female stockbroker shed her business suit against a background of plunging sales graphs. In another, a nude girl in a dungeon struggled ineffectually but erotically with her chains, no doubt in a plea for the release of political prisoners. Another routine recalled the days of Sputnik. Two stately young women, near enough to twins, dressed in identical gold lamé helmets and not much else, tussled in a space capsule. It reminded me painfully of Roger Vadim's high-camp film of the comic strip *Barbarella*, but for the first time Milou's attention was engaged. She nudged me.

"The shoes," she murmured.

"What about them?"

I could see that their impossibly high-heeled sandals, soles as thick as wedges of wedding cake, must be hell in low gravity.

"Christian Louboutin."

"Who?"

She waved a hand in dismissal of my ignorance. How could I have failed to see that, for women, sex was so not the point of shows like this, compared with the fact that one of the leading lights of shoe design provided the footwear?

Decouflé had benched some old favorites, including the number in which a girl crawled all over the red velvet couch designed by Salvador Dalí in imitation of the lips of Mae West. Also gone was "Lay, Laser, Lay," for decades a high point of the show. To the sluggish pulse of Oscar Benton's "Bensonhurst Blues," the dancer, lit by a fan of blue laser light and wearing only string (and little of that), slithered and writhed on a slowly revolving circular platform tilted toward the audience. I last saw it performed by a girl who, in a Crazy Horse tradition, hid her identity behind a pseudonym, in her case Roxy Tornado. (Others have included Akky Masterpiece, Lily Paramount, Rita Cadillac, Lana Polar, Lova Moor, and my favorite, Fuzzy Logic.) My appreciation even survived meeting Roxy in the flesh and finding a rather ordinary young woman from, of all places, Palmerston North, New Zealand.

Celebrity dancers compete to appear at the Crazy. Arielle Dombasle, the almost scarily thin wife of philosopher Bernard-Henri Lévy, did a season there, as did celebrity stripper Dita von Teese. The show so fascinated Toni Bentley, for ten years Balanchine's star at the New York City Ballet, that she asked Bernardin for a job in the corps de ballet. He turned her down, not for lack of talent but because she didn't conform to his rule that all dancers be five feet four inches tall and identically proportioned. Their physical features, from eyes to crotch, had to line up precisely. "Like a painting," he explained, "like a Modigliani, everyone the same." He did allow her backstage, where she collected some makeup secrets. Dior No. 004 gave the girls a uniform creamy pallor, while their pubic triangles proved, like the moustaches of Charlie Chaplin and Groucho Marx, to be Leichner Black greasepaint.

Beside me, Milou watched in silence. Not everyone was so respectful. Although the audience remained in darkness, an occasional overspill of light from the stage illuminated the banquettes where a gleam of thigh suggested some couples, finding the show insufficiently erotic, were making their own entertainment. I'd once brought to Le Crazy a friend more used to raunchier performances. As the troupe marched out for another demonstration of close-order calisthenics, he yelled "Take 'em orf!" Other patrons shushed him indignantly. "It was like we were listening to Beethoven's late quartets!" said my friend.

After the show, Milou and I crossed the avenue for cocktails at the George Cinq.

Since my last visit, its lounge and inner courtyard had undergone a lavish makeover. Flower arrangements six feet tall erupted like fountains of color, and the pianist who used to vamp on Porter and Gershwin now played Lionel Ritchie. One felt as dwarfed by the setting as any tourist at Notre Dame or the Eiffel Tower. To do something as conventional as drink in such a place seemed a failure of imagination. At the very least, a full orchestra should materialize in the courtyard, now relit as artfully as a stage set, and a choir rise on a hidden elevator to sing extracts from *Les Misérables*.

A waiter with the air of a high-class mortician placed something like a footstool beside Milou's chair. Before I could ask her what it was for, she put her handbag on it. A handbag rest? What next?

"What did you think?" I asked Milou as we browsed the bulky drinks menus. There were so many essays on the hotel's décor, history, and distinguished clientele that it was hard to find any reference to cocktails at all.

"The show?" she said. "Pretty, I suppose. Like watching arty shop window displays, except that the mannequins moved." She turned another page of the menu. "What do you suppose goes into a Dunmore Sour Mulata?"

"Not sexy, then?"

She thought for a moment. "I liked the shoes."

Two blond girls took the table next to us. Still in their teens, they spoke London English, but softly. Though their black dresses and jewelry were discreet, both appeared somehow soiled.

At this time of night—but really at any time of the day or night, if you could believe the gossip—most unaccompanied women in these hotels were prostitutes. Could these girls be double-teaming for the tired businessman looking for Something a Little Different? If so, their style was a triumph of marketing and packaging: just discreet enough to attract attention but casual enough to provoke.

I was almost ready to start a conversation when a willowy woman in impossibly high heels and a crimson evening gown swayed by on the arm of a shorter, older man. She passed before we turned our heads, so we didn't see her face. It didn't matter. It was impossible to watch anyone else, a fact of which both the man and woman were fully aware. *Something in the way she moves* . . .

"Now *that* . . . ," said Milou respectfully, "is sexy!"

Later she emailed me. "If I were you, I'd forget the Crazy and just describe the cocktail bar and that woman in Valentino red."

She was right, of course.

And she was right about the shoes.

Part Four

27

Underworld

Do you know what you remind me of? The subway.
You're all silk, and you jingle when you walk, and yet
with all that chi chi you make me think of the subway.
Isn't that funny? And potato chips, and coffee on the
boulevard.

Pepe le Moko to Gaby in *Algiers*

There are as many ways to see Paris as there are Parisians, but seeing them en masse is where patterns emerge. And for that, no place is better than Paris's subway, the métro.

Some call the métro the bloodstream of Paris but it's more like the nervous system, and we passengers those fizzing zips of energy that carry messages from organs and extremities to the brain. Blood is homogenous; nervous energy is not. Each impulse is separate, private, a quantum of being. And the line where those quanta

*Charles Boyer as Pepe le Moko and Hedy Lamarr
as Gaby in* Algiers

flow in the most intriguing variety is the deuxième—
the number 2 line.

I was a stranger to the deuxième until I spent a week
minding the flat of a friend in Montmartre. Most days I
walked the streets, constantly surprised by a new corner
of the city.

Plastered to the haunch of the butte of Montmartre, the

eighteenth arrondissement has an architecture and lifestyle all its own. Along rue Marcadet, diamond-shaped lots from the days when these were market gardens or *guinguettes*— beer gardens—have dictated apartment blocks with parallelogram floor plans. What does it do to your brain to live in a room with no right angles? Maybe it explained the pale faces that stared out from a few windows: shut-ins, with nothing to do but watch the world go by.

Caught in the gaps between these habitations, like bits of gristle in a set of crooked teeth, businesses survived that you seldom see in more prosperous districts: plumbing supply shops, shoe repairers, molders of false teeth, and undertakers, along with makers of funerary monuments. The *Montmartrois* joke that once you visit the *dixhuitième*, you stay forever—because it's the arrondissement with the most graveyards.

My friend lives on rue du Square Carpeaux, a short, wide, sloping back street, surfaced—unusually for Paris—not with cobbles or asphalt but brick-shaped blocks of slick gray stone resembling flint: another attempt by the restless city to find the ideal paving material. As the blocks aren't cemented in place, grass grows in the cracks, attracting small birds that peck for insects. As there's no through traffic, the street often echoes to one of the rarest of all sounds in Paris, birdsong.

Perhaps it was their twitter that lured me out that warm Saturday morning—that and knowing that a big street market was taking place around Père Lachaise cemetery. Admittedly, it was on the far side of the city. But it was in just such obscure markets that treasures surfaced.

Plotting my trip on the métro map, I decided to take the deuxième. The moment I passed between the pillars of Hector Guimard's art nouveau entrance, I was aware of a different métro to the lines I knew.

Looking down the platform, I saw more black and brown faces than white, and Muslim women in the head scarves frowned on in the central arrondissements. In tourist Paris, police and métro staff excluded panhandlers from the stations and severely limit buskers. Up here, where tourists seldom come, they relaxed the rules. Musicians also felt no need to skulk. One waited with a battered accordion, another with a clarinet and an old luggage trolley to which he'd taped an ancient beat box.

We all boarded the same train. Its doors had barely closed before the clarinetist's beat box started to rap a muffled rhythm. His medley of favorites, precisely calibrated to the distance between stops, included nothing French, and, just as we slowed into the next station, ended hurriedly with "My Way." Beat box still tap-

tapping, he circulated with his Styrofoam cup, ignored by almost everyone, and stepped off onto the platform.

At almost the same instant, the accordionist, having waited his turn, struck up "El Choclo," a staple of tango dancing since the turn of the nineteenth century. In 1952, someone added English lyrics to make it "Kiss of Fire."

Give me your lips, the lips you only let me borrow
Love me tonight and let the devil take tomorrow.

Who danced the tango anymore? Nobody in tourist Paris. But in its strut and pose, the dance belonged on the deuxième. I half expected each man in the carriage to grab the woman next to him, haul her to her feet, and execute a few spirited steps along the center aisle.

No other métro line had ever induced these fantasies in me. The deuxième, I was discovering, was the line of love, or at least of lust. If Paris had a streetcar named Desire, this was it. How could it be otherwise, when the line begins at Porte Dauphine, center of Paris's *échangiste* culture, and curves across the tenderloin of nineteenth-century Paris—Pigalle, Clichy, Menilmontant—to expire on Place de la Nation?

Even the posters on the platform walls sang a siren

song. One promoted a show of Tamara de Lempicka's florid art deco portraits. The one next to it announced a new variation in computer dating: an online hook-up service for wives wanting "a little bit on the side." The posters showed, from the back, a woman wearing something between a wedding dress and a white waspie. She was hiding one hand behind her, and the fingers were crossed.

In 1967, Jean-Luc Godard made *Two or Three Things I Know About Her*. The main character is a housewife who moonlights as a prostitute in her home. Obviously some things about Paris don't change, although these days the amateurs are taking over. Internet services such as Croisé dans le Métro (Crossed on the Métro) and the Craigslist section called Missed Connections offer a chance to meet the person whose eyes you met across the aisle on the 7:43 from Gare du Nord, but most such attempts don't survive the moment. A spark flashes between two people . . . then each goes back to his or her iPhone or paperback of Gide.

Paris could be fertile ground for a French version of the Japanese *chikan densha* or "pervert train." Certain Tokyo clubs provide facsimile subway carriages, complete with station announcements, even authentic noises and vibration, and staff them with suitably dressed men and women who cooperate in acting out your fantasy. Hearing of this reignited a vivid moment from a visit to Japan with my blond American wife. As we traveled back to our hotel late one night on a jolting train, a dark-suited *sarariman*, so drunk he could barely stand, stared at her hair for three stations before finding the courage to reach out and tenderly stroke it.

A s the train glided into each station on the deux-ième, a recorded voice spoke its name. Until now, that voice had been male, but at the stop after Place de Clichy, it became female.

"Blanche," she murmured, then, after a beat, *"Blanche."*

The effect was seductive. The first time, she spoke the name flatly, politely, the second time more intimately, as if responding to a question only she heard.

"Blanche." ("What station did you say, mademoiselle?") *"Blanche."*

And abruptly I was back in the film *Algiers*, listening to Hedy Lamarr, the beautiful tourist, flirting with gangster Charles Boyer, who must remain inside the native quarter, the casbah, or die in the streets that surround it.

"Do you know Paris?" she asks.

"Do I know Paris?" he replies incredulously. "La rue Saint-Martin . . ."

"Le Champs-Elysées . . ." she responds.

"Le Gare du Nord . . ."

"L'Opéra . . . boulevard des Capucines . . ."

"Abbesses . . . rue Montmartre . . . boulevard de Rochechouart . . ."

"Rue Fontaine . . ."

Then, both together, "La Place Blanche." They laugh. "What a small world."

That world was even smaller than he knew. It was at a café on Place Blanche that André Breton convened the daily séances of the surrealist group, to whom the busy, brilliantly lit intersection possessed mystical significance. "Nights here do not exist," he said, "except in legend."

At the next stop, a surge of new passengers washed in our first beggar. Towering, unshaven, saddled with a backpack, and apparently blind, he moved slowly among us, staring over our heads as he mumbled his appeal— a ritual, worn featureless by years of repetition, all sense had been rubbed away. He carried no cup nor did he hold out his hand. Even if we wanted to give him something, there was no way to do so. He ambled down the center aisle, as indifferent to us as we were to him— Eliot's Tiresias from "The Waste Land" who "bestows one final patronizing kiss, And gropes his way, finding the stairs unlit."

The next beggar made up for his reticence. As short as the other was tall, he hustled in off the platform, shoving through the standing passengers. His arms were bare. Loose gray trousers were rolled above his knees and bunched around his hips and crotch. His left leg and both dirty feet were bare, his left foot turned inward and half over, so that he walked on the outer edge. Apparently deformed hips imposed a swiveling, crablike rolling gait with, yet, a Popeye arrogance.

Sidling up and down the crowded carriage, he kept up a litany of complaint and appeal, eloquent in its simplicity.

"Help me, please . . . help me . . . I need help . . . help me . . . please . . ."

We who habitually ignored beggars felt discomfited. A few fumbled for coins. When the train halted at Place de Clichy, he didn't get off but, unusually, returned down the carriage for one last circuit—a lap of honor?

As he passed, I pressed a euro into his hand. It earned me no thanks—just a moment to study him more closely. No ordinary beggar this. His hair was trimmed, as was his short beard. Facial hair was unusual in a beggar, who ran mostly to stubble. Neither stale sweat nor food stains soiled the cotton knit shirt. As he turned away, I studied his legs and feet. The twisted one didn't appear deformed or withered. There was no callous where the skin touched the ground. As for the hips, his trousers were so bunched that one couldn't see them.

Was that intentional?

And weren't his trousers a little too baggy for normal wear? Where the belt cinched them tight around his waist, the cloth gathered under the strap. What if he straightened up, let the trouser legs fall to his ankles, placed the soles of his feet flat on the ground? I was almost certain he could walk quite normally. This was no invalid. This was a performer. We'd been treated to a skilled mime. Perhaps, like Neville St. Clair in the Sherlock Holmes story "The Man with the Twisted Lip," he made enough from begging to support a family in the suburbs and live like a gentleman. I was glad to have contributed the euro—if not from compassion, then appreciation.

28

Scent of a City

A woman who doesn't wear perfume has no future.
COCO CHANEL

RATP, the agency managing the métro system, spends a fortune on perfume every year. How else to neutralize the odors of burning rubber, hot oil, and ionized air? Not to mention the smell of commuters in their hundreds of thousands, and the effluvia of the homeless who haunt the more remote stations, pissing into any convenient drain.

They first tried in the 1990s with Francine, a mixture of natural plant extracts: eucalyptus, lavender, mint. It flopped in trials. For their second attempt, code name Madeleine, they abandoned the "green" agenda in favor of those synthetic aromas used by most modern *parfumiers*: vanilla, jasmine, lily, citrus, rose. It did the trick. Since 1998, Madeleine has been poured onto métro stations at the rate of 1.5 metric tons a month.

I'm used to it now and only notice it when a polished look to the asphalt on the platforms shows that the cleaning crew has passed by in the night. Like the increasingly common announcements in French, English, Italian, and German to mind the gap and keep an eye on your belongings, it's integral to the commuters' daily equation of *métro, boulot, dodo*—métro, work, sleep.

France didn't invent perfume but it refined it. In the Middle Ages, the French, born gardeners, became skilled at using steam and oil to isolate, extract, and concentrate fragrances. It took 440 pounds of lavender to produce just over 2 pounds of essence, but those who lived in the stinking cities of the day were glad to pay, while the rich didn't hesitate to invest in the secretions of animal musk glands and ambergris, a waxy material excreted by sperm whales. Diluted and mixed with other aromatics, these produced fragrances of a carnal pungency appropriate to the courtesans of Versailles, which, under Louis XV, became "the perfumed court." But the price of smelling good was a bad reputation. By the 1900s, for any woman to wear a scent other than a dab of lavender or rosewater marked her as "fast."

This changed early in the twentieth century. The perfumer Jacques Guerlain, strolling on a summer evening by the Seine (or, in some versions of the story, along a country path), was struck by "the spectacle [of] nature bathed in a blue light, a profoundly deep and indefinable blue. In that silent hour, man is in harmony with the world and with light, and all the exalted senses speak of the infinite." Supposedly this revelation inspired him to create the perfume known as L'Heure Bleue—the Blue Hour.

"There was a peculiar smell that emanated from the coffeehouse terraces of Montparnasse," wrote author Frederick Kohner of Paris in the early 1920s, "and I only have to close my eyes to bring it all back to me; the rich mixture of cigarette smoke, garlic, hot chocolate, *fine à l'eau* [cognac and water], burned almonds, hot chestnuts, and—all pervading—the strong scent of a perfume that had just become the rage of Paris— L'Heure Bleue."

Though his date is wrong—L'Heure Bleue first went on sale in 1912—Kohner is right that its arrival signified a fundamental change in the use of personal fragrances. The marketing of the perfume was as inventive as its fabrication. Painters and photographers had long recognized the "blue hour" when daylight becomes dusk as the moment when natural light is at its most flattering. But no distiller of fragrances, however masterful

his technique, had ever claimed to capture anything so fleeting as atmosphere. What Guerlain saw in his epiphany was not so much a method of catching magic in a bottle as a way to make money.

Synthesizing such aromas as vanilla and jasmine cost far less than animal secretions and flower oils. Able to produce complex fragrances at a much lower price, perfumers could spend more on presentation. Guerlain enclosed a few spoonfuls of L'Heure Bleue in a molded and gilded flacon of Baccarat crystal with a stopper representing an inverted but hollow heart. Not accustomed to expensive receptacles, women enjoyed the container as much as the scent. Janet Flanner wrote of pioneer perfumer François Coty that he "perceived perfume as something in a lovely bottle rather as merely something lovely in a bottle. He presented scent as a luxury necessary to everybody."

Guerlain used the L'Heure Bleue bottle for Mitsouko in 1919. Every manufacturer now grasped the importance of the container. The midnight blue bottles of Evening in Paris by Bourgois were soon familiar worldwide. Even Chanel bowed to the market and licensed her Chanel No. 5. Coty transformed the scent business by pioneering mass marketing. He hired glassmaker René Lalique to design his containers. At the same time, he expanded into low-priced soaps, powders, and eaux de toilette. Lalique's designs, reproduced in enamel and crystal for the carriage trade, were adapted to paper and cardboard. Coty exported vigorously, in particular to the United States, with powders and colognes scented with such fragrances as L'Origan (oregano). Now that women everywhere could enjoy L'Origan at a modest price, its round orange boxes with their Lalique design became famous.

A new popularity of fragrances for men fed the market even more. While some nineteenth-century perfumes, such as Guerlain's Jicky, were aimed at both sexes, men avoided accusations of effeminacy by using toilet water, eau de cologne, or aftershave—all diluted forms of perfume. A dash of bay rum, made from bay leaves and other aromatics macerated in alcohol, was thought manly, as was Old Spice, launched in 1938 and marketed through the Boots pharmacy chain in Britain.

No manufacturer, however, produced the dream of all perfumers—a scent that would attract all men. In 1937, Elizabeth Arden suggested her fragrances had male appeal because they made women smell like a rolling Kentucky landscape, but "outdoorsy" seems to attract only those types of men, largely the creation of advertising agencies, who appear in glossy magazines promoting scotch whisky and are seen either stroking a red setter with a Purdey shotgun over their shoulder, or lounging in a paneled library, crystal decanter at their elbow and leather-bound first edition in their lap.

Something more visceral was needed, a scent that reached down into the medulla oblongata and caressed the very core of maleness. Perfume historians Luca Turin and Tania Sanchez proposed the most convincing candidate. "After years of intense research, we know the definitive answer. It is bacon."

29

The Nose That Knows

*And the LORD said unto Moses, Take unto thee sweet
spices, stacte, and onycha, and galbanum; these sweet
spices with pure frankincense: of each shall there be a
like weight: And thou shalt make it a perfume, a confection after the art of the apothecary, tempered together,
pure and holy: And thou shalt beat some of it very small,
and put of it before the testimony in the tabernacle of the
congregation.*

Exodus 30: 34–36, *King James Bible*

The last time I remember a fragrance ravishing my
senses had nothing to do with women. On a hot
night in Los Angeles, visiting an old apartment house
near the beach at Santa Monica, I walked into the
courtyard, to be engulfed in the perfume of *Cestrum
nocturnum*—night-blooming jasmine, also called Lady
of the Night. Banks of it loomed out of the darkness on

both sides. A fountain a few yards away, tiled in orange and brown, crawled with thousands of ladybugs. They tumbled and struggled in a frenzy. Nothing living could resist this stifling blitzkrieg of scent.

Such an epiphany was rare, since I have the olfactory equivalent of a tin ear. My nostrils had practically to touch the surface of wine before I got even a whiff of bouquet, and if Marie-Dominique asked my opinion of her new perfume, her hair had to be tickling my nose before I smelled anything.

I could tell the difference between perfume and no perfume, but not much more. When a woman held out the wrist on which she'd just dabbed something and asked, "What do you think of this?" I wasn't so stupid as to say, "Don't ask me. I can't smell a thing." A selection of evasions existed, and I became adept at their use. "Mmmm . . . interesting. Is it French?" worked most of the time. If it looked too expensive, I'd also had some success with "It's lovely—but is it you?"

If I liked anything about perfume on women, it was the *idea* of it: the element of calculation it implied. Men generally want to be accepted for what they are, women for what they've become. Men don't enjoy dressing up. Especially we dislike wearing ties or cufflinks or fragrances bought by loved ones. Each woman, on the other hand, is an individual work of art, a creation, intended to exhibit her skill at presentation. Speaking for myself, but I think also for many men, I find the most attractive element of female beauty its artificiality. And to that, perfume is crucial. In celebrating gardens, Louis Aragon, the most sexually ambivalent of the surrealists (his taste for white leather trousers rather gave him away), compared them to women and, in doing so, coined some phrases that, to me, apply equally to feminine beauty. In particular, he captured the appeal of a woman meticulously dressed, perfumed, and posed to impress.

> *Your very contours, your artless abandon, the gentle curves of your rises and hollows, the soft murmur of your streams, all make you the feminine element of the human spirit, often silly and wayward, but always pure intoxication, pure illusion.*

A few years ago, I visited the headquarters of Fragonard in Grasse, on the Côte d'Azur. One enters the building from the street and then, since it's built on a cliff, descends level by level, past its offices, its museum, its workshop, to the lowest, which houses a shop the very air of which seems to have been entirely replaced by perfume.

As the *vendeuses* let me sniff the various essences and fragrances I'd promised to buy for my wife and daughter, I could only think of the fortunate husbands and lovers to whom these women went home. Drenched in perfume day after day, how did they smell? Of what did they taste? Women who wish to make themselves particularly alluring to their lovers drink quantities of tea perfumed with orange or jasmine. If they consume enough—a full pot, according to the best advice—the scent manifests itself in their . . . um, juices. Was it the same with these girls? Did the fragrances they sold penetrate into their very cells? If I hadn't been due in Antibes the next day on a film shoot, I would happily have devoted a few days to finding out.

Intellectually, I knew how Paris should smell: anise, absinthe, roasting chestnuts, coffee, all mixed with the rival perfumes worn by women in the street. In practice, I smelled almost nothing. Occasionally, the tang of burning charcoal catches my nose as I pass Giovanni at his longtime pitch outside Deux Magots. I sometimes smell burning sugar from a crêperie if the cook is, just at that moment, smearing the pancake with honey or Nutella or if a maker of *barbe à papa* was spinning colored sugar into what we called fairy floss as kids. Otherwise, I might as well have my head in a sack.

In planning a smell walk, I accordingly recruited an expert. Kate has turned her finely tuned sense of smell into an area of expertise. Sniffing out rare odors with the precision of a truffle hound, she traps them on absorbent paper for incorporation into "smell maps" that delineate a city not in geographical highs and lows but as overlapping zones of plant, animal, and chemical scents.

As a blind person exists in a world of touch and sound, Kate swims in a world of smells. In person agile and lean—as a hobby she runs marathons—she evokes both a forest animal and the dogs that hunt them. She'll freeze "on point" as her nose traps a transient thread of smell.

"Ah! Get that? Roses . . ."

Her nose swings like a compass needle to point at a bush of yellow *Desprez à Fleurs Jaunes* in a tiny garden across the street.

"And . . . pizza?"

Swiveling back, she nails the overweight citizen of Perth Amboy, New Jersey, ambling past us, munching on a slice of *quattro stagioni* ("hold the anchovies").

Montmartre seemed a good place to start. Calculating that it would be easier to begin at the highest point of the butte that dominates Paris to the north and work our way down, we arranged to meet on Place du Tertre.

Regarded as the village green of Montmartre, this gently sloping cobbled square with a few stoically enduring trees is drenched in history. When Baron Haussmann modernized central Paris, demolishing most of its slums, many of the dispossessed migrated up here, finding shelter under any available roof. Mills, workshops, and sheds became homes. With no municipal money for proper roads, goat tracks and even staircases were transformed into streets.

Montmartre became a popular weekend hangout for slummers. Being outside the city walls, it levied no tax on alcohol, and the police were either too indifferent or too scared to crack down on street crime, prostitution, abortionists, drug dealing, and cabarets presenting the sort of songs and dances never heard or seen on the *grands boulevards*.

In 1871, the end of the Prussian siege, the fall of Emperor Napoleon III and the defeat of the French army left Paris briefly ungoverned. Into the power vacuum rushed the citizens of this, the most rebellious of its districts, who gathered on Place du Tertre to declare the city a socialist enclave, the Commune. To back it up, they had a hundred cannon, purchased from their own pockets when it looked like the Prussians would invade the city rather than just besieging it.

The Commune introduced votes for women, pensions for widows and orphans, free education, separation of church and state, the suspension of usurious debt, enlightened working conditions, and staff takeovers of failing businesses. Opera and drama were performed free and the royal art galleries opened to the public for the first time. Delirious with freedom and the spring, the *Montmartrois* danced in the streets and sang a song written a decade before, "Les Temps des Cerises"—The Time of Cherries.

> *When we sing of the time of cherries*
> *Even nightingales will be gay, and mocking blackbirds*
> *Go wild in celebration*

The cherries about which they sang weren't the plump variety from Spain that flood French markets each summer in a tide of lipstick red. Bigarreau Napoléon cherries are heart-shaped rather than round. Yellow-pink, they bruise easily. Their flesh is more tart than the sugary Spanish fruit, and their season shorter. When the Bigarreau make their appearance in the markets in July, it's a signal of more than a change in seasons. For a few weeks, Parisians are reminded that their city was once considered worth fighting, even dying, for.

The first troops sent to put down the rebellion mostly came from Paris, many even from Montmartre. They refused to fire on their own people but shot their commanders instead. After two generals had been killed by their own men, the army withdrew. Wiser heads within the Commune knew that, like the cherries, the uprising could not last. Fresh troops brought in from the south had no loyalty to Paris. As Communard factions bickered, traitors admitted the army through the gypsum mines under the hilltop where the cathedral of Sacré-Coeur would eventually stand. Tens of thousands of Communards were slaughtered or deported to New Caledonia, and the last verses of *Les Temps des Cerises* became a lament.

> *It is short, the time of cherries*
> *Coral-pink fruit one picks in dreams*
> *I will always love the time of the cherries.*
> *It's a time I keep in my heart—*
> *An open wound.*

Although Place du Tertre seemed a good place to start our smell walk, Kate and her friend Kevin, who's come over from London to watch her at work, flinched, as I did, from the mob filling the square.

In 1898, André Citroën, determined to prove his cars could go anywhere, drove one up winding rue Lepic and triumphantly parked here. It would be the last time anyone drove or parked easily in Montmartre. Today, a combination of one-way systems and massive tourism has made the streets impassable to any vehicle less flexible than the toylike train that trundles tourists around the butte, towed like children in an amusement park.

Traditionally, it was at the restaurant Mère Catherine at 6 Place du Tertre that Russian Cossacks in March 1814, flooding into Paris after the defeat of Napoleon, demanded to be served *bystro!*—quickly—and created an enduring term for a café. They'd be pleased to see that the row of postcard sellers and fast-food stalls that used to occupy the center of the place had become a cluster of sit-down restaurants, above which a few surviving trees poked their heads like drowning giraffes. The alley between where the center restaurants ended and those fringing the square began was cruised by predatory street artists who, if you let them catch your eye, homed on you with sketch pad and pastels, hungry to imprison you on paper.

As a miasma of hot oil, burned sugar, and sweating flesh threatened to drown Kate's sense of smell, we retreated down rue Lamarck to the frontage of Sacré-

Sacré-Coeur by Raymond Thiollière

Coeur. Though tourists had colonized the tumble of steps below the cathedral, the evening breeze swept the air clean and clear, showing the valley of Paris at its best. This view never disappoints.

One can't say the same about Sacré-Coeur, one of Paris's most familiar sights but among the least visited. Once one has toiled up here by métro, funicular, and on foot, it seems a waste of the effort to simply visit a church, particularly one as odd as this one, perched on the hilltop like a cluster of button mushrooms or a particularly unflattering hat.

The pale bulbous domes evoke nothing ecclesiastical. A 1920s caricature depicted them as penises squirting indiscriminately over the city—which, given Montmartre's scandalous history, is closer to poetic truth. The artist of that image was Raymond Thiollière, one of the talented soreheads who traditionally flock to Montmartre. He worked in woodcuts, a particularly unforgiving technique. The artist uses a chisel to gouge shallow lines into a block of wood, then inks the surface and prints off a copy. Some artists soften its almost brutal graphic style by using colored inks and finer tools, but Thiollière didn't bother. Even his gentler images, such as a view of Place du Tertre in the 1920s, an empty square inhabited by a few ambling locals, convey an air of despair, while most verge on madness. He died in 1929, in the same anonymity in which he'd lived. The single website to take notice of his work comments: "As far as we can discover, this artist wrote nothing, gave no lectures nor interviews of importance, nor has any correspondence been published. This page awaits any information." None has been forthcoming.

Looking up at the dusty gray façade of Sacré-Coeur, Kate asked, "Should we go inside?"

"If you like," I said. "Perhaps we'll find the odor of sanctity."

Does virtue smell better than sin? The nuns and priests around whom I was raised were as prone as any sinners to body odor and the furtive fart. Certain saints, even after death, were supposed to give off a perfume, usually compared to violets.

It was less common among the living, though the British playwright Alan Bennett sometimes caught a whiff of what appeared to be a heavenly odor. In one case, a waiter at an outdoor restaurant in Rome, it turned out to be particularly powerful aftershave, but when Bennett detected it while visiting the country home of Alec Guinness, he was convinced he'd found in that mild, courteous, and modest actor the true scent of holiness—until, walking by a grove of balsam poplars, he realized it was their buds that gave off the delicious fragrance, a scent so intense that the Bible celebrates it as the balm of Gilead. It may even have been the myrrh, which, with gold and frankincense, the three wise men brought as gifts to the infant Jesus.

Sadly, Sacré-Coeur held no balm of Gilead. The one overpowering smell was paraffin wax. In every alcove, before every statue, and at both entry and exit doors, banks of candles blazed. Two Euros bought a tiny candle in a metal cup that burned for about fifteen minutes. For ten, you could have a red or yellow glass tumbler filled with enough wax for an hour. I half expected to see the image of Jesus on the inside of the glass, with the information that, for a small additional sum, you could take the glass home as a souvenir, but Sacré-Coeur drew the line at that degree of commercialization—at least for now.

I was tempted to light a candle for the lost innocence of this ancient tradition. "It reminds me of childhood birthday cakes," Kate said. We both knew she was looking for a bright side in the pervasive commercial gloom. During my Catholic boyhood, each church had only one bank of candles, payment was optional, and the air was perfumed with that distinctive merging of heat and honey that signifies burning beeswax—the closest approximation, to me anyway, of the true odor of sanctity. Back then, the church had insisted that ecclesiastical materials be as close to nature as possible. Not only was beeswax natural; it yielded a pure golden light and that pleasant scent. American author Helen Mackay, writing about Paris under German occupation, articulated a formula for the fragrance I'd hoped to find: "the smell that so belongs to old French houses, of beeswax and musk and secrets." But paraffin burned slower and cost less, so beeswax candles went the way of meatless Fridays and the Latin mass.

As we were ready to leave the cathedral, an idea struck me. While no scent would cling to stone, the wood screening the entrance and exit might, over a century, have soaked up some odors. Putting our noses to the dark oak, we sniffed for a distinctive signature. Did the faintest trace linger of the incense burned here in decades of high masses, the floral arrangements of a thousand funerals? Then Kate nudged me. A large security man was eyeing us. We escaped into the twilight and the more familiar though less saintly smells of sweat and sore feet.

30

Gardens of the Night

We must cultivate our own garden. When man was put in the garden of Eden he was put there so that he should work, which proves that man was not born to rest.
VOLTAIRE

W e should have a garden," said Marie-Dominique thoughtfully when we moved into our Odéon apartment. She might as well have said, "We need a cow up here." The terrace, two meters deep and fifteen long, had all the horticultural promise of a four-lane freeway. Floored in galvanized steel, it was fenced off from the sheer drop to the street by some utilitarian square-section bars in Sing Sing green. Two ancient rose trees, stark as crucifixes, languished in cement pots. Add the fact that it was six floors up a serpentine staircase, with no elevator, and the task seemed hopeless.

But never underrate a Parisian's sense of purpose. Today, rosebushes and conifers screen the view over the roofs toward Notre Dame. Revived by food and pruning, the old roses explode annually with giant pink blooms that wave out over rue de l'Odéon, to the wonder of the sixth arrondissement. Our cat Scotty performs daredevil gymnastics on the trunk of an acacia five meters tall. The metal floor has disappeared under Astroturf and the fencing behind ivy, honeysuckle, and grapevines. Irises bloom in pots, and a minijungle of annuals flourishes in an Edwardian galvanized steel bathtub recovered at midnight from a *benne*, as the French call a dumpster.

Getting that tub into the car, back to the apartment, and up the stairs was just one triumph in two decades of sweat and swearing, bad backs, blistered hands, and incredulous "You must be kidding!" stares as deliverymen with sacks of potting mix glared up the stairwell from the ground floor. Nor did the exposed location welcome these new arrivals. In summer we occasionally needed to drench the plants twice daily against a sirocco that coated the leaves with fine red dust from the Sahara, while frost killed a lively wisteria and even shattered the inch-thick stoneware of the antique pickling pot in which we'd planted it.

But now we couldn't live without the garden. In spring and summer, the French windows are almost permanently open, turning the terrace into an extension of our living room. Croissants and coffee in the morning, drinks in the evening, coffee after dinner—all taste better taken in leaf-dappled sunlight amid the fragrance of growing things. And on summer evenings, when we water the plants in the velvet night, Voltaire's "We must cultivate our garden" seems more than simply advice to mind your own business. Maybe, as much as we are looking after our garden in the sky, our garden is looking after us.

Such thoughts place us in good company. French intellectuals who've never been closer to horticulture than watering a window box go into rhapsodies over the significance of gardens. Even Louis Aragon, arguably the least practical and high-minded of the surrealists, exploded with almost incoherent enthusiasm at the mere thought of them.

Among your flower beds and box tree alcoves, man strips off old habits and returns to a language of caresses, to a childishness of water-sprinkling. He himself, as he whirls round with wet hair, is the sprinkler in the sun. He is the rake and the spade. He is the chip of rock. Gardens, you resemble otter-skin sleeves, lace handkerchiefs, liqueur chocolates.

Since Paris is a city of apartments, almost none of which have gardens, or even terraces, what Aragon and most French writers usually meant by "gardens" were public parks. In his case, he was talking about the Parc des Buttes-Chaumont, on the southeast edge of the city, in the unfashionable nineteenth arrondissement. The fifth largest park in Paris, more spacious than even the

Luxembourg Gardens, it preserves a sense of the period when it was built.

In the 1850s, Napoleon III, determined to rival his much more gifted uncle, Napoleon I, set out to make Paris an imperial capital. He commissioned Haussmann's reconstruction of the city and the building of such grandiose monuments as the Opéra and Buttes-Chaumont. Massive earthworks were required to mold this former garbage dump into a park. Aragon was right to compare it to a box of expensive chocolates or a coat of otter or seal, all signifiers of bourgeois status. Its artificial waterfalls and plaster grotto, the faux-Greek temple perched on a cliff top, its rustic shelters and swooping tree-shaded walks, the outdoor theaters, teahouses and restaurants show how the designers sternly brought the environment to heel. This is nature as fashion accessory, tamed and adapted to act as a background to those who stroll in its leafy artificiality.

Putting God in His place is a Parisian specialty. Nothing, not even nature, may stand taller than the people of Paris. The more natural something seems, the more likely it is to have been created. Pass through the Luxembourg Gardens just after the gates open in the morning, and you may see teams of gardeners lifting whole flower beds and, after pumping superheated steam into the earth to cleanse it of weeds and pests, slotting into their place entirely new blocks of blooms, already brought to perfection in some suburban hothouse. New lawn is unrolled like carpet. Aged trees are pulled like rotten teeth and youthful ones planted in their place. In summer, palms and fruit trees boxed in green-painted crates are trundled out of the Orangerie on forklifts, which, in turn, carry back the evergreens to sit out the hot weather in cool and calm.

All over the city, tiny parks and squares replicate this sense of nature under control. Shop windows onto French thought, they invite reflection. Henry Miller, passing through Place de Furstenberg by day and night from his hotel on rue Bonaparte, saw more than one lesson in the stately chestnuts and plane trees of this secluded little square—circle, actually—tucked away between boulevard Saint-Germain and rue Jacob.

Looks different now, at high noon. The other night
when I passed by it was deserted, bleak, spectral.
In the middle of the square four black trees that
have not yet begun to blossom. Intellectual trees,
nourished by the paving stones. Like T. S. Eliot's
verse. Here, by God, if Marie Laurencin ever
brought her Lesbians out into the open, would be

the place for them to commune. Très lesbienne ici.
Sterile, hybrid, dry as Boris' heart.

Miller's free-fall prose sometimes needs footnoting. The paintings of Marie Laurencin, mostly languishing girls, pale, disdainful, and expressionless, do seem made for the boudoir, and are seldom seen out of doors. As for T. S. Eliot, his reticent poems often evoked lonely cityscapes.

Let us go then, you and I,
When the evening is spread out against the sky
Like a patient etherized upon a table;
Let us go, through certain half-deserted streets,
The muttering retreats
Of restless nights in one-night cheap hotels

Henry was probably right to suggest that Furstenberg, a square that's actually a circle, would be a suitably ambiguous location for them to consort.

My favorite among Paris parks is the Vert-Galant, the tiny point thrust into the current of the Seine from the end of the Île de la Cité. When I lived on Place Dauphine, on the other side of Pont Neuf, I often came here at night, communing—or hoping to—with the spirit of

Henry IV, nicknamed Le Vert Galant, a "green gallant," a man who remains virile despite his age. His equestrian statue up on street level still stands guard over the park named for him.

Though a lively community of rats keeps the casual walker away at night, nocturnal wanderers find their scuttling no more disturbing than the rush and suck of dark waters and the clack and swish of bare willow fronds in the night wind. If any isle was ever full of voices, this is it. Jacques de Molay, grand master of the Knights Templar, was burned at the stake here in March 1314. More recently, the ashes of situationist philosopher Guy Debord, formulator of psychogeography, were thrown into the Seine from this park. But if there are voices, they are the kind that lull rather than alarm—murmurings as soporific as Caliban's voices, that "if I then had waked after long sleep, will make me sleep again."

One is closer here to the water than at almost any other point along the island, a temptation to which hundreds have succumbed over the centuries. The presiding spirit of the Vert Galant isn't King Henry but an unknown girl whose drowned corpse, according to legend, was, sometime in the 1880s, fished out of the river directly opposite. A plaster cast taken of her calm, almost

dreamy face, christened *L'Inconnue de la Seine*—the unknown girl of the Seine—inspired scores of novels, stories, and poems. The writer Richard Le Gallienne saw her features as "shining, like a star among the dead. A face not ancient, not modern; but of yesterday, to-day, and forever." In his story "The Worshipper of the Image," a young artist buys a copy of the mask, takes it home, and explains the legend to his mistress. Laying it on a couch, he tucks a black cloak around it. "The image nestled into the cushion as though it had veritably been a living woman weary for sleep." Recognizing she can never compete with this dead ideal, the woman drowns herself.

Proving that history repeats itself, first as tragedy, then as farce, *l'Inconnue* has enjoyed an unexpected modern reincarnation. In the 1950s, Norwegian toy-maker Asmund Laerdal chose hers as the face of Re-susci Anne, the plastic figure used to demonstrate such lifesaving techniques as mouth-to-mouth resuscitation. Since then, more than 300 million people have kissed those dead lips.

If there are parks that truly speak to me, that breathe that unique scent which no visitor to Paris ever forgets, they are not Buttes-Chaumont or the Luxembourg or even the Vert-Galant but small anonymous suburban spaces fenced in behind railings, with a few benches, often with a children's playground at one end and an area cov-ered in asphalt for playing ball games. Trees hide them from the surrounding buildings—or perhaps shield the buildings from the sight and noise of children at play. In winter, foliage falls, blows, and gathers in corners—the dead leaves about which Jacques Prévert wrote in one of his best-known poems and most popular songs.

I scoop up the dead leaves,
Of memories and regrets

But my faithful, silent love
Smiles always, and thanks life.

A different writer from another country captured the attraction of the winter landscape for me while I was still at school. Kenneth Grahame wrote *The Wind in the Willows* in 1908. Supposedly a fable for children about animals living along a river in rural England, it's actually an elegy for an England that the Great War would sweep away forever. Grahame wrote about nature with a clear-eyed lack of sentiment. A description of his tentative and unassuming hero, Mole, coming to terms with a leafless world sums up to me all the minimalist pleasures of empty parks and bare trees. Neither Ernest Hemingway nor Graham Greene ever did it better.

It was a cold still afternoon with a hard steely sky
overhead, when he slipped out of the warm parlor
into the open air. The country lay bare and entirely
leafless around him, and he thought that he had
never seen so far and so intimately into the insides
of things as on that winter day when Nature was
deep in her annual slumber and seemed to have
kicked the clothes off. Copses, dells, quarries and

all hidden places, which had been mysterious mines for exploration in leafy summer, now exposed themselves and their secrets pathetically, and seemed to ask him to overlook their shabby poverty for a while, til they could riot in rich masquerade as before, and trick and entice him with the old deceptions.

Part Five

NIGHT 5:
SIGHT

31

The Black-and-White Man

Then one day I fell in with a photographer. He knew the city inside out, the walls particularly. . . . Our favorite resting places were lugubrious little spots. . . . Many of these places were already familiar to me, but all of them I now saw in a different light owing to the rare flavor of his conversation.

HENRY MILLER, *Tropic of Cancer*

Given the importance of books in my life, it's ironic that I should have been born in Australia, at that time among the least literary nations on earth. Or perhaps that very hostility to the printed word drove me, perversely, to embrace it with even more passion. By the time I was eleven, my books had exceeded an accumulation and could fairly be called a collection. Reading a description of moving house in *My Family and Other Animals*, the memoir of naturalist Gerald Durrell, I recognized a fellow soul in his elder brother, Lawrence, later the author of *The Alexandria Quartet*. "Larry was accompanied by two trunks of books," wrote Gerald, "and a briefcase containing his clothes."

I loved reading but I loved books almost as much. Their look, their smell, their weight enshrined, to me, the worth that others found in religion, in bricks and mortar, even in relationships. A book could be friend, lover, family, priest, but more reliable than any of these. With books, one could wall off the world. In their shelter, a calm prevailed more profound than that of the stars or the sea.

I never doubted that a night walk in Paris based on sight would revolve around a book. But what book? I lived at the heart of the world's most literary city, in the very building where *Ulysses* and *Finnegans Wake* came into being: a building visited by the authors of *The Great Gatsby*, *The Sun Also Rises*, and *The Wasteland*. Any one of those masterworks might anchor a promenade. And yet . . . none fitted my need for a book intimately associated with our *quartier*, even our street.

There were a number of false alarms. A store almost opposite the Sorbonne sold mainly overstocks, usually of glossy picture books more at home on a coffee table than a library. As I was looking in the window, my eye was snagged by a title. *La Maison Que J'Habite*—The House I Live In.

On the cover, a dark, winged shape—a *papillion de nuit,* or moth—hovered above an antique oil lamp. By inking out details of the design on the wings and adding a suggestion of slanted eyes, the photographer had reduced the moth to a malevolent silhouette.

I knew this image. It appeared in 1935 in the magazine *Minotaure,* edited by surrealism's founder, André Breton. I'd even met the man who took it. Some tangles in the web of probability are too flagrant to ignore. As I stepped into the shop, I was already reaching for my wallet.

P aris waits for you," goes the saying.

Some people take this as a promise, an assurance that the city drowses, Sleeping Beauty–like, on the banks of the Seine, awaiting the mutual awakening of a kiss. To others, it implies a trap. If Paris waits, it is in ambush.

Hemingway called the city "a moveable feast." He meant in part that there was no set time of life in which to encounter it. In childhood or one's dotage, it remained equally welcoming, its gates seductively open, offering a glimpse of . . . what? To find out, you had to push them open and peer inside. Those who did sometimes got a shock. In the film *An American in Paris*, Leslie Caron suggests to Gene Kelly that Paris is a city that helps you forget. He disagrees. "No, not this city. It's too real and too beautiful. It never lets you forget anything. It reaches in and opens you wide, and you stay that way." A growing body of fiction shows strangers falling victim on the streets of Paris to *femmes fatales*, swindlers, serial murderers, even vampires and ghosts.

That's how I arrived in Paris—as one of the emotional walking wounded, a casualty of desire. After a chance meeting in Los Angeles with a former lover, I abandoned California in a matter of days and followed her to France. The French call so abrupt a decision a *coup de foudre*—a thunder clap. Most of its victims come to their senses as the rumbles fade. Within a few weeks they begin to sense the strangeness of France and its innate hostility to the unknown, and head for home.

I was fortunate. My companion turned out to be the love of my life. Seeing this, her family generously educated me in its idiosyncrasies. In the process, I discovered a culture and way of life inexhaustible in variety and charm. But my story was exceptional. Most new-comers flee within a few months, cursing the French in general, and bad-mouthing in particular meddling in-laws, pigheaded bureaucrats, and the maddening intricacies of the language.

We who stick and stay are in good company. The gifted of Europe have been fleeing to France for centuries. Before World War II, every cultivated European learned French, not English. As frontiers were redrawn after World War I, former Russians, Serbs, Croats, and Transylvanians who had become, with a stroke of some politician's pen, citizens of new countries, preferred, rather than learning another language, to embrace their intellectual and spiritual second home, Paris.

Gyula Halász was a Transylvanian of Hungarian parents. When he first came to Paris, he adapted his name phonetically, to Julius Halash, but abandoned that for a pseudonym taken from the name of his home town in the Carpathians. The Austro-Hungarians made it a summer resort called Kronstadt. After World War I, it reverted to the old name, Brassó or Brasov, and so Gyula Halász became the man from Brasov—Brassaï.

Appropriately for someone from the same region as Count Dracula, Halász felt most at home in the Paris night. Often with his friend, the American writer Henry

Miller, he prowled the streets, first writing about, then photographing those people who emerged only after dark. The book I'd just bought cataloged a show of his photographs staged by a museum in Nancy. The curator had rounded up his more obscure and enigmatic images: not people but abstract patterns of cobbles on a wet street, graffiti gouged into plaster walls, a single metal chair in the Luxembourg Gardens, closeups of steel needles ranked in a paper sleeve or water beaded on a leaf.

At home, I shelved *La Maison Que J'Habite* among other books about Paris between the wars. It fitted neatly next to his better-known *Paris La Nuit* and Henry Miller's autobiographical *Quiet Days in Clichy*. Brassaï illustrated both with images of prostitutes, petty criminals, drug addicts, and homosexuals, all apparently at ease in the sort of clubs and bars that only opened after midnight. For years, we assumed he simply snapped these people as he found them during his nocturnal wanderings. In fact he staged his pictures, recruiting photogenic subjects and placing them, carefully lit, in the proper atmospheric setting. Spontaneity held no interest for him. Each image was as meticulously calibrated as a fugue.

My own Brassaï photograph has a place of honor, next to first editions of *Ulysses, A Farewell to Arms, The*

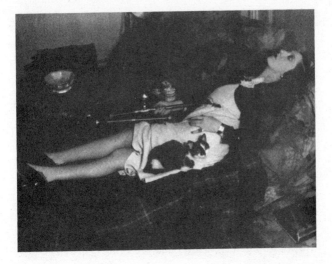

Making of Americans, and *Tender Is the Night*. Taken in the late 1930s, it appears in *Paris La Nuit*. A fashionable matron in an art deco dress drowses in a Paris opium den or fumerie. Beside her are the pipes she's just smoked. A black-and-white cat stares out at us, incuriously. The image captures everything I ever read about the effect of opium: the extinguishing of all sense of time and of every desire. The woman drifted in an eternal Now—a green thought in a green shade . . .

The fumerie he visited was probably Drosso's, the most fashionable of these establishments and the one most patronized by expatriates. For Caresse Crosby, wife of Harry Crosby and his partner in the Black Sun Press, it was "the one place in Paris where the sumptuous rapture of the east was evoked in the ease and luxury of the surroundings." I once spent a couple of days searching for the site of this legendary temple of dreams. Historians who give the address as 30 allée du Bois obviously hadn't bothered to consult a street guide, since no allée du Bois exists. In the 1920s, there had been, however, an avenue du Bois de Boulogne, which, in 1929, was renamed avenue Foch in tribute to the marshal of World War I.

Wide and tree-lined, avenue Foch runs from the Arc de Triomphe to the Bois de Boulogne. The Rothschilds had a mansion here. So did the composer Claude Debussy. With the Bois, preferred playground of the demimonde, on one edge and, on the other, Porte Dauphine, notorious rendezvous point of *les partouzeurs*, one can hardly imagine a more select or secluded address. A characterless modern apartment building now occupies No. 30, but nearby mansions, anonymous behind their spiked railings, suggest the discretion in which Drosso's took such pride.

On arrival, clients exchanged their clothes for silk kimonos. (Brassaï's self-portrait in *Paris la Nuit* shows him reclining in just such a robe.) After that, explained

Caresse Crosby, "we stepped in upon a scene from the Arabian Nights. The apartment was a series of small fantastic rooms, large satin divans heaped with pillows, walls covered with gold-embroidered arras, in the centre of each room a low round stand on which was ranged all the paraphernalia of the pipe. By the side of each table, in coolie dress, squatted a little servant of the lamp. The air was sweet with the smell of opium." For important clients, Drosso, who dressed in a kimono decorated with a giant butterfly, prepared the pipes himself. "The soft clouds wooed one's body," wrote Caresse, "winding and unwinding its spell, holding one in a web of lustless rapture. Smiling, one relaxed and drowsed, another's arms around one, it mattered little whose."

Brassaï thought it only polite, as a visitor to the fumerie, to sample a pipe or two. After doing so, he asked some clients if they were prepared to talk about their use of the drug. "Of course!" said a woman identified only as "a beautiful actress." She went on: "I'm proud to smoke. They say that after a while opium will make you thin, weaken you, ruin your mind, your memory. Rot! Look at me, and tell me frankly, am I not beautiful and desirable? I've smoked opium for ten years and I'm doing all right."

Even in 1979, the photograph of the woman in the

fumerie cost more than I could afford, but it never occurred to me not to buy it when a London gallery presented a small Brassaï retrospective. Almost before the
gallery owner folded acid-free tissue around the print
and placed it in a stiff card portfolio, I'd grabbed it and
squeezed into the circle of admirers clustered around
the expressionless little man whose features appeared to
droop in terminal weariness.

Holding the print by its edges, I said breathlessly (I
wince at the memory), "I just bought this."

He looked at me and the picture without expression.
Perhaps the corners of his mouth turned down a little
more.

"Thank you for your patronage," he said. Optimis-
tically, I interpreted his tone as formal politeness. not
sarcasm.

"Would you mind signing it?"

"With pleasure."

He didn't sound so much pleased as resigned. Someone handed him a pencil and he scribbled his signature
on the verso.

I debated telling him that I'd visited his home town,
now in Romania. Sent there by the U.S. State Department to speak at a conference, I'd found myself extolling
Hollywood horror films to an audience of steely-faced

teachers of English, mostly middle-aged ladies, any one of whom could have doubled for Margaret Hamilton, the Wicked Witch of the West in *The Wizard of Oz*. Ten minutes into the talk, a thunderstorm worthy of Frankenstein rolled in from the Carpathians. I could imagine a scientist in a nearby tower channeling its lightning into the artificial man he'd sewn together from corpses or a giant bat sweeping into the hall and, alighting, metamorphosing into Count Dracula himself.

Wisely, I spared Brassaï this recital. His memories of Brasov were probably as jaded as mine of Junee, the town where I grew up. Reminding him of those days could only induce the warning signs James Thurber listed in his *Guide to the Literary Pilgrimage*—"the stiff posture, the horrible smile, the inattentive monosyllabic interjection, and the glazed expression of the eye." Fellow fugitives, we had made our way independently to Paris. Let others look for a place in the sun. We had something far more treasurable—our place in the shade.

32

Frenzy and Darkness

*I announce to the world this momentous news item; a
new vice has just been born, man has acquired one more
source of vertigo—Surrealism, offspring of frenzy and
darkness.*

LOUIS ARAGON, *Paris Peasant*

don't know why it took me so long to see the ideal
book as a model for my "sight" walk. Like the Cluny
tapestries, it was probably too close.

For a while, *Paris La Nuit* or *Quiet Days in Clichy*
topped my list. That I'd met Brassaï and visited his home
town hinted at some mystical link, but it felt a little too
obvious. Instinct told me the correct book would make
itself known.

That it should have done so on the opposite side of the
world came as a surprise. It happened at the end of an expedition to the Pacific Northwest with a friend, Nicholas.

"To awaken quite alone in a strange town," remarked the travel writer Freya Stark, "is one of the pleasantest sensations in the world." In my case, the town was Portland, Oregon, the time 2:00 a.m. It was raining a torrent and, in the next room, my traveling companion appeared to be expiring to a terminal cough.

A combination of constant rain and his diet of coffee and tobacco had laid Nicholas low with bronchitis. By the time we reached Portland, heading for Los Angeles, his bark sounded like someone shoveling coal in the furnace room of hell. Fortunately, a fellow dealer, Charlie, took us in, dosed Nicholas, and sent him off to bed while he and I sat up and talked shop.

Over the second bottle of Bordeaux, Charlie said, "I might have something for you." He disappeared into the back room, returning with a book bound in frog-green cloth. In eighty years, the gilt of its art deco lettering had faded to a sickly yellow, but I could still read the title. *The Last Nights of Paris.* It was Philippe Soupault's novel of walking in Paris by night, in the version translated by American poet William Carlos Williams.

"Do you have it?" Charlie asked.

"I've read it," I said, "but I've never seen the first edition."

"Don't bother about the penciled price," he said. "We can make a deal."

Few artistic groups have provided so much sheer fun and creative excitement as the surrealists. They dignified chaos, revered violence, relished dreams, celebrated sex, loved movies and jazz. In short, they were my kind of people.

In London during the 1950s, jazz singer George Melly, a new member of Édouard Mesens' surrealist group, eagerly attended the weekly meeting and supper, traditionally known as a séance, held in the upstairs room in an Italian café.

Mesens encouraged me to read my poems aloud. In one, there was a line "You are advised to take with you an umbrella in case it should rain knives and forks." One evening I collected a great deal of cutlery from a sideboard and, on reaching this image, hurled them into the air. The effect was very satisfactory, the noise formidable, but while the Surrealists' applause was still resounding in my gratified ears, the proprietor rushed up the stairs and ejected us all.

Melly quickly found that obeying one's surreal-ist instincts could even save your life. On tour with a jazz band in Manchester, he was ambushed in an alley by some young thugs. Armed with razors and a broken bottle, they advanced toward him.

I subconsciously did the only thing that might work, and it did. I took out of my pocket a small book of the sound poems of the Dadaist Kurt Schwitters, explained what they were, and began to read.

"langerturgle pi pi pi pi pi
langerturgle pi pi pi pi pi
Ookar.
Langerturgle pi pi pi pi pi
Ookar.
Rackerterpaybee
Rackerterpaybay
Ookar . . ."

Slowly, muttering threats, they moved off. If I'd pleaded or attempted to defend myself, or backed against the wall with my arm over my face, I think I'd have had it.

The more time I spent thinking about night walks, the more I returned to the surrealists. No group walked as tirelessly or with such purpose. André Breton based *Nadja*, his novel of *l'amour fou*, around a series of walks in pursuit of a woman who obsessed him. Louis Aragon became an urbane and articulate explorer of both boulevards and back alleys in *Paris Peasant*, and, most enigmatic of all, Philippe Soupault's *Last Nights of Paris*, part poem, part murder mystery, and a progenitor of *film noir*, took place in streets I could see from my terrace.

The surrealists had left their *griffes* everywhere. On walks through Montparnasse, I always paused by a small hotel on rue Delambre; a plaque in the entrance announced that André Breton had lived there for a time before losing patience with Montparnasse's triviality and moving across town to the more businesslike Montmartre.

I took these eccentrics so much for granted that it never occurred to me that not everyone knew who they were.

"What was this surrealism anyway?" one client asked. "Some kind of cult?"

In certain ways it did resemble a cult. Breton certainly behaved like a guru, to the extent that some members called him, not particularly kindly, "the pope of surrealism." In other ways, it was more like a club, and quite a small one. There were seldom more than a dozen

*Some of the surrealists, 1930. Back row: Man Ray, Hans Arp,
Yves Tanguy, André Breton. Front row: Tristan Tzara, Salvador
Dalí, Paul Éluard, Max Ernst, René Crevel.*

seriously creative members, and the numbers kept dwindling as Breton imposed some new rule.

Breton reminded me of the childhood game Simon
Says. The leader orders "Simon says, Stand on one
leg!" and those who obey stay in the game but those
who do something else or follow a command not directly from Breton are out. Some of his orders were
easier to obey than others. His first commandment required that everyone must attend the daily séance on

Place Blanche. There was only one acceptable excuse for absence—lust. So powerful was the urge to be with a woman—Breton detested homosexuality—that it could not—must not—be resisted.

Subsequent directives were more demanding. He insisted, for instance, that none of the group accept payment for their work; it compromised their creativity. Some dropped out on this account, but the majority remained—to be reduced still further by his order in 1926 that all join the Communist Party, since its aims coincided most closely with those of the group.

Most Parisian members agreed, with the exception of Philippe Soupault, whom Breton ejected, even though he was one of the cofounders of the movement. Members in foreign countries, however, risked more than excommunication. In a monarchy, to be a communist automatically made you an enemy of the state. Some surrealists from the Balkans and Eastern Europe had to flee for their lives.

"But what did the surrealists *do* exactly?" asked my visitor. "Paint, write, perform?"

"Well, all of those, to some extent. But mostly they talked, and . . . well, played games."

"Games? You mean, like football?"

I tried to imagine the surrealist football team—

something to which only Monty Python's Flying Circus could do justice.

"No. Most of the original surrealists were writers. So they played word games mostly."

Their favorite was Exquisite Corpses, a version of the children's parlor game in which one draws the head of an animal, folds the paper and passes it to others who add the body and legs, with the whole creature only revealed when the paper is unfolded. In the surrealist version, players compiled sentences, not drawings, each person adding a word. They named the game for an early success: "The exquisite corpse will drink new wine."

The American walker shook his head in disgust. "Ya ask me, they sound as crazy as a sack fulla assholes."

He wasn't entirely wrong. In the 1920s, when the movement was at its height, plenty of people agreed with him. The surrealists championed chance, play, spontaneity—everything serious literature detested. In its place, Breton preached the *acte gratuite*—any action performed on the spur of the moment, with no thought of consequences. As the ultimate example, he proposed emptying a pistol into a crowd, indifferent to whom it killed. While none of the surrealists took their beliefs that far, they didn't flinch from violence.

They attacked nuns and priests in the street and interrupted the performances of any person who dared use the term "surrealist" without permission. After each excess, Breton wrote a polite note to the victim, emphasizing the sincerity of their motives. And to show that they too had suffered, he decorated the corner of each letter with a drop of blood.

Janet Flanner, Paris correspondent of *The New Yorker,* found the surrealists disgraceful and fascinating in equal parts.

Surrealism was basically founded on the principle that art should not be beautiful but on the contrary should shock and dismay the eye of the beholder. Another of its concepts was violent anti-Catholicism, usually demonstrated by the Surrealists insulting priests and spitting on nuns in the Saint-Germain streets. Interest in the ancient study of dreams was also a Surrealist fundamental, as was devotion to Leon Trotsky and Freud, and, in Surrealism's sadistic physical practices, street brawling was considered an essential. The Surrealists had their own club table facing the door of the Deux Magots from which vantage a seated Surrealist could conveniently

insult any newcomer with whom he happened
to be feuding, or discuss his plans to horsewhip
the editor of some belligerent anti-Surrealist
newspaper for having mentioned his name or,
worse, having failed to mention it.

But the surrealists were, on the whole, more mischievous than malicious, with a precocious interest in what came to be called pop culture. Surrealism challenged the prevailing aesthetic. Before them, few intellectuals saw merit in genre fiction, jazz, or movies. In particular they admired the film serials directed by Louis Feuillade about master criminal Fantômas and a gang calling itself the Vampires. As its voluptuous, acrobatic (and anagrammatic) leader Irma Vep, the actress known simply as Musidora flaunted her sexuality in a daringly clinging black body stocking with a stiletto strapped to one thigh.

That Feuillade, a stolid family man of stern rightwing principles, saw neither poetry nor sensuality in his creations just made his achievement that much more delicious. At a time when nobody, not even the authors of the original stories that inspired the films, took these thrillers very seriously, the surrealist Robert Desnos wrote a long poem dedicated to the masked gangster.

He was inspired by the cover of that first novel in the series, showing a gigantic figure in evening dress and a black domino mask staring down on a sleeping Paris, bloody dagger in hand.

Stretching his immense shadow
On the world and on Paris,
Who is this grey-eyed ghost
Who appears in the silence?

It must be you, Fantômas,
Who raises himself above the roofs.

At its most trivial, surrealism was George Melly fooling with knives and forks, Marcel Duchamp inverting a urinal and calling it *Fountain*, or the group indulging in Cadavres Exquis.

But surrealism also opened literature to the idea of free association and stream of consciousness. It inspired Breton and Soupault to improvise *Les Champs Magnétiques*—The Magnetic Fields—a series of texts using "automatic writing," a form of word jazz that riffed on language. Batting words, phrases, and images back and forth, they were unconcerned with whether they "made sense." Readers puzzled over such passages as:

A great bronze boulevard is the shortest road.
Magical squares do not make good stopping
places. Walk slowly and carefully; after a few
hours you can see the pretty nose-bleed bush. The
panorama of consumptives lights up. You can hear
every footfall of the underground travelers. And
yet the most ordinary silence reigns in these narrow
places.

The more perceptive realized that a doorway had opened onto a new and disturbing landscape; the magnetic fields of a Europe left dangerously unstable by the world's first industrial war.

And all this took place not a hundred yards from where I lived. Could that be coincidence? To me, it seemed more like fate.

33

Bound for Glory

*Books are not made for furniture, but there is nothing
else that so beautifully furnishes a house.*
HENRY WARD BEECHER

Could it really be thirty years since I first en-
countered Paul Delrue? For once, the cliché "I
remember it as if it was yesterday" rang true, since I
could still recall that day in 1979 and the crafts shop
next to the cathedral in Chester where a book, bound
in blue and brown leather, caught my eye.

The woman in charge took it out of the glass case,
but with a puzzled look, wondering why anyone could
be interested in such an exotic object. In her estimation,
hand-bound books ran a very long last to neckties, T-
shirts, key rings, and other souvenirs.

The moment I held the book, even before I opened
it, I knew I was going to buy it. My interest might

have been less had the binder chosen *Traditional Crafts of the Outer Hebrides* and not the 1923 first edition of D. H. Lawrence's *Sea and Sardinia*. It wasn't the text that attracted me, but rather what the neatly typed card inside described as a binding of "tan goat skin, colored Oasis onlays, gold tooling and colored edges."

What made it so particularly satisfying? Not, as I said, the content. Collectors of first editions want books in a condition as near as possible to that in which they left the warehouse. In collecting terms, rebinding rendered it almost valueless. Besides, Lawrence was not among my enthusiasms. I shrank from his emotionalism and passion, preferring the cooler, drier insights of Graham Greene.

All this counted for nothing, however, beside the elegance, discretion, and sheer craft of the binding. I marveled at the expertise with which two of the colored woodcut illustrations by Lawrence's friend Jan Juta were reproduced in colored leathers inlaid into the front and back covers and another in miniature on the spine. And when I opened it at last, how naturally it lay on the counter, with none of the tendency of similar books to close of their own accord, a sign of a binding fitted too tightly to the book. Its perfection was that of a sonnet or

a fugue: modest, formal, self-contained, in and of itself perfect.

If this were a movie, a simple dissolve would link my paying for *Sea and Sardinia* to the moment when I walked up to the door of the binder's home. In practice, it was more complicated. Unusually, he didn't identify himself with a label on the pastedown, so someone at the shop must have provided his contact details. And his combined cottage and workshop in the depths of the Welsh countryside didn't exactly invite the casual drop-in.

Even after we met, it took some time to get to know Paul Delrue. The word "reticent" hardly begins to describe his personality. We'd met a number of times before I learned he'd been brought up in a Catholic home for foundlings and only reunited with his birth mother when he was fifteen. There was something doubly Dickensian about first the decision to have him learn a trade, and then have him apprenticed to one of the most antique of them all, bookbinding. By 1967 he'd won so many prizes and acquired such a reputation that he was invited to join the team in Florence working to save and restore the rare books damaged when the Arno flooded in the winter of 1966. The precision and craft in the binding of *Sea and Sardinia* began to make more sense.

That was the first of many such visits, and a succession of commissions. My collection soon contained Delrue bindings of Richard Llewellyn's *How Green Was My Valley*, Dylan Thomas's *Portrait of the Artist as a Young Dog*, Dashiell Hammett's *The Maltese Falcon*, and many other books, not to mention sensitive restorations of some favorite books where my copies, though early and rare, were often battered. He gave new life to distressed editions of Wilkie Collins's pioneering crime novel *The Woman in White* and to my favorite Dickens novel, the austere *Bleak House*.

I knew Paul still worked as a binder. We'd exchanged messages over the years, but it was some time since I'd commissioned anything. It was time to renew our relationship. I emailed him to explain my idea.

My next book is called Five Nights in Paris, *and deals with the Paris night in all its aspects—scent, sound, taste, vision, and touch. I'm thinking it would be interesting to commission a binding of a book that deals with the same topic. It would be an ideal departure point to talk about the French love of books—and my own, come to that. There are various candidates. For instance, I have many volumes of the first UK edition of Proust in the Scott-Moncrieff translation.* Cities of the Plain *and* Within a Budding Grove *have substantial nighttime passages. Another possibility is* Ulysses *and its wonderful "Nighttown" episode. I have various printings of the Shakespeare & Company edition, although since the city in that case is Dublin, it's an outside choice. There's Djuna Barnes's* Nightwood, *Paul Éluard's* Capitale de la Douleur, *and Philippe Soupault's* Last Nights of Paris, *a quite sinister surrealist vision of the Paris night.*

Even before he responded, I knew what book we would choose. I took my copy of *Last Nights of Paris* from the shelf. The texture of the cloth, somewhere between suede and well-rubbed velvet, felt greasy; disturbing to the touch; unworthy of Soupault's text or Williams's translation. *Then change it*, murmured an inner voice. I wrapped it hurriedly and walked round to the post office before logic could change my mind. It only occurred to me as the clerk stuck on the stamps that I was indulging in an *acte gratuite*.

34

Waiting

The thing about Paris, it's a great city for wandering around and buying shoes and nursing a café au lait for hours on end and pretending you're Baudelaire. But it's not a city where you can work.

MALCOLM MCLAREN

While I waited for Paul to work his magic on *Last Nights of Paris,* I recruited friends to help me explore some of Paris's darker corners.

"It's like a uterus," Ingrid said.

I looked around the Café du Rendez-Vous on Place Denfert-Rochereau. On the other side of the large room, across the lanes of brown-varnished tables, a decidedly nonuterine barman polished glasses. If the cavernous and crepuscular café in this corner of southern suburban Paris had any resonances with the female reproductive system, they were too obscure for me.

"How do you figure that?"

Ingrid's blue-gray eyes had a knack of appearing to look right through my brain to read the secrets written on the inside of my skull.

"The uterus is like this." She held up her fist. "But as the child begins to grow, it swells." Her long fingers unfolded. "Which is what happens in here. By lunchtime," she said, adding her other hand and spreading them outward from her navel, miming the swelling belly of pregnancy, "it will be bulging."

I drank the rest of my noisette in silence. If you make friends with a psychotherapist, you expect conversations like this.

It seemed entirely appropriate to our talk that a network of underground limestone quarries riddled the ground beneath our feet. We were dealing, after all, with the Darker Side of Paris. Across the road, a queue had formed at the booth where one paid to descend into them.

Baron Haussmann's teams of stonemasons, returning from demolishing medieval Paris, would load the empty wagons with skeletons exhumed from former graveyards and plague pits, and re-inter them in the galleries from which they'd cut the stone. Pious men, they arranged the remains with respect, using professional skill to create walls of bones as they did of bricks; a course of ulnas, one of pelvises, a third of skulls. The bones of 6 million French men and women lay under our feet.

Ingrid had never visited this corner of our adoptive city, so I'd volunteered to take her down the winding cement staircase and lead her, Virgil to her Dante, through what a warning over the lower entrance called "the kingdom of Death."

In the nineteenth century, the tunnels, misnamed "catacombs," became a convenient hideout for criminals and political plotters, who left signs of their passing gouged into the soft stone. Eccentrics of a melancholy disposition asked to be buried down here. One encounters every few hundred meters an ancient marble slab, too stained by time to make out the name.

Obeying the same reverence that caused them to order the bones, masons cut niches to make shrines, made paths for the increasing number of visitors, and fenced off ponds where water had filtered down through the stone. The miners who cut the galleries refused to drink their water, so cleansed of impurities by the stone that it appeared to them unnaturally clear. Students of the mining and geology schools traditionally dunk new graduates head-down into one of these still pools.

Once mining ceased, mushroom growers moved in. For years, the catacombs produced hundreds of tons each year of the bulbous white buttons which, though they grow almost anywhere, are still known as *champignons de Paris*.

During World War II, both the Germans and the French resistance used the tunnels. Only a few years ago, explorers of an old network nearer the Seine found an entire cinema dating from the 1940s, complete with comfortable chairs and projection equipment. When they returned a few weeks later to explore in more detail, everything had disappeared.

For this, one can blame a group who call themselves *cataphiles*—lovers of the catacombs. It's an open secret that certain manholes scattered around the area will admit you to the tunnels after hours. Graffiti on the walls show that taggers know most of them. In one huge chamber, known as *La Plage*—the beach—an elaborate copy, many meters long, of Hokusai's famous woodcut "The Breaking Wave" decorates the walls.

But if the catacombs are meant to be scary, they fail. Crowds of people visit them every day and emerge a couple of hours later more amused than chastened. Conceptions of the underworld have moved on. Jean-Paul Sartre articulated the opinion of many when he wrote in his play *Huis Clos*, "Hell is other people." To the existentialists, Hades wasn't walls of bones but the more horrific walls of a waiting room where nothing ever happened and one was doomed to repeat the same mistakes into eternity.

Sartre spelled this out more fully in one of his rare screenplays, *Les Jeux Sont Faits*—The Chips Are Down. It belongs among the most depressing films of 1947, a year notable for downers—something I can verify from experience, since that was the year I began to understand grown-up movies. Though I didn't experience its languid hopelessness until much later, *Les Jeux Sont Faits* slotted perfectly into 1947, easily punching its weight with, for instance, *Nightmare Alley*, in which Tyrone Power, as the "geek" in a traveling carnival, bites the heads off live chickens.

Though obviously set in Nazi-occupied France, *Les Jeux Sont Faits* respects prevailing sensibilities by changing the location to an unnamed fascist state. Eva, wife of a high official, is poisoned by her husband at the same moment as a traitor shoots down resistance leader Pierre. They meet for the first time in the afterlife, which Sartre imagines as identical to our own, except that the dead of all ages continue to inhabit it, unseen by us, the living.

A few of these revenants blow on the ashes of life, hoping to revive a spark. One old marquis, hanged two centuries ago, volunteers to act as a guide for Eva and Pierre, but breaks off to pursue an attractive woman. "I never get very far," he says with a shrug, "but it passes the time." Most of the dead, however, just hang about, looking over our shoulders as we defecate, fornicate, and pick our noses—a disturbing prospect. One can imagine Sartre composing these scenes at Brasserie Lipp, Deux Magots, or the Flore, always wearing the same dingy brown raincoat, forever fantasizing of being watched by everyone who ever ate there.

An amiable old lady seated with her cat behind a huge ledger records the names of new arrivals and directs them to the door leading to eternity. I'd known dozens like her: clerks in regional town halls, receptionists at dingy hotels.

When Eva and Pierre sense a growing mutual attraction, the same woman explains that, in such rare cases, people can be returned to life for twenty-four hours. If their love flourishes, they will be restored to the living. It ends in tears, of course. Eva's friends scorn her working-class lover: when he calls on her, a servant sends him round to the tradesman's entrance. Both become too caught up in their old lives to think of love,

Les Jeux Sont Faits. *Charles Dullin as the old marquis, Marcello Pagliero and Micheline Presle as Pierre and Eva.*

and so die at the instant their twenty-four hours expire. Back in the afterlife, they drift apart to join the other ghosts, weary with seeing people repeat, century after century, the same errors.

At 10:00 a.m. in the Café du Rendez-Vous, the hours of café crème and croissants were coming to an end. The last lingering office workers left, heading for their desks. Already most of the tables were set with the *couverts*— knife, fork, spoon, plate, paper napkin—that indicated lunch. At the nearest of the square wood-paneled columns supporting the six stories above us, a waiter in a long white apron climbed onto a chair. Erasing yesterday's specials from the blackboard (*côte du porc roti, purée maison, tarte aux pommes*), he began, using the almost unreadable cursive of all waiters, to chalk up today's menu.

After lunch would come the tourists, footsore after a few hours of trudging through the catacombs. After they'd taken a load off their feet and headed back to their hotels, they'd be followed by the businessmen who, for the price of an espresso or two, used the café as their office, spreading their papers across the table. Later still, around five in the afternoon, the predinner period would begin. Here's how it was described by Soupault in *Last Nights of Paris*.

> *The café was taking a little nap. The aperitif hour had passed, and that of chocolate and sandwiches had not yet come. The waiters stood about with bowed heads and dangling arms. A few had seated themselves, looking much like those statues that receive gold medals at the salon and adorn public squares—useless, motionless and out of date.*

By comparing the café to a uterus, Ingrid had imposed a newer vision—one that took root and invaded my perception. The autumn sun's rancid yellow light now appeared denser, as if an amniotic fluid had stealthily insinuated itself until we were, all of us, both in the café and outside, immersed. In the street, young women, uniformly dressed in the black and brown wool and leather chic of early winter, wove purposefully through the traffic—like antibodies, I thought, alert for any infection. And that crocodile of preschoolers, hands linked, eyes unfocused, moonily abstracted, direction-less? One could almost imagine them as a chain of molecules in red mufflers and knitted gloves . . .

"Voulez-vous autre chose?"

I hadn't noticed our waiter, but his presence at my elbow jolted me out of the fantasy. We were suddenly back in an ordinary café and, as far as he was concerned, an impediment to the business of preparing for the lunch trade.

"Oh, rien, merci. L'addition, seulement."

He slapped it down before I finished asking.

Ingrid stood up.

"Must go pipi."

But she didn't move. Instead, as if the view from this new perspective stimulated a different perception, she went on, "This is the only café where anyone offered me money for sex."

These observations of hers used to throw me. Now I barely paused in counting coins to pay for our coffees.

"Recently?"

"Oh, no. Years ago. In my twenties."

"Lot of money?"

She did a swift mental calculation.

"Corrected for inflation, about six hundred euros."

"Generous."

"I'm pretty sure he would have paid even more. He drove a Porsche. Had a vast apartment in the sixteenth."

"If you saw his apartment, I assume you accepted."

She gave me That Look again. I thought for a second that she might actually answer the question. But only for a second. Ingrid's life was a twenty-four-hour-a-day demonstration of the principle of "need to know."

"Won't be long," she said. "Then we can go look at your skeletons."

My eyes followed her to the steps that led down to the toilettes. Stately, long-legged, an American woman totally in charge of herself and the world. But when exactly had they become *my* skeletons?

I was left alone at the table with two empty coffee cups and the little dish on which the waiter had left our bill, torn across to indicate it was paid.

Why do waiters so seldom figure in memoirs of

Paris? They would have been the Frenchmen with whom expatriates most often came in contact. One of the few to write about them did so in 1916.

British journalist E. Bryham Parsons painted a dreary picture of their existence, particularly those who worked in the *bouillons*—large cheap restaurants that offered "working men's dinners" and stayed open late, if not all night, to catch the last night owls and the first early birds.

Desiring some gruyere cheese, I called the waiter. He was holding himself more or less upright in a great archway which led into the adjoining room. I presently approached and touched him. He was fast asleep. He explained he generally worked until 3 in the morning. "3am—it's too late," he said, "particularly if you live in Paris." I believed him. The all-night business, so charming to Englishmen let out on a holiday from genuinely soporific London, where a restaurant found open at three in the morning would be visited with a crushing fine, makes Jacques, the waiter, or Henri, the rough-and-ready garcon of the bouillon, a dull boy. The following Saturday, I went in again. The place seemed utterly deserted. The Parisian waiter does

*not snore, but I knew that not far from me, on
the floor, on the stairs leading into the kitchen, or
huddling themselves for warmth and comfort round
some stove in the basement, the waiters slept that
fearful sleep which knows no fixed hours, which is
as full of shocks as some terrible nightmare, and
which may be banished any instant by the terrible
cry, 'Café, s'il vous plait!' which, breaking in on
their dreams, will bring the whole dozen of them to
their feet, staggering, gasping, and blinking before
a single insignificant customer.*

As Ingrid returned, I put two euro coins on the table.

"For two cafés?" she said. "You're already paying fifteen percent service, remember."

"I know."

"Then why so generous?"

I looked off into the shadowed interior of the Rendez-Vous. How many waiters of other eras were hanging around unseen, even more bored in death than they had been in life? How many former clients, awaiting *l'addition* that would never come? Hell is other people.

"For the ghosts," I said.

35

Exquisite Corpse

He calleth to me out of Seir, Watchman, what of
the night? Watchman, what of the night?
*   The watchman said, The morning cometh, and*
also the night.

   Isaiah 21:11–12, *King James Bible*

For years, my friend Kevin and I had talked of taking a surrealist walk around Paris, following in some of their footsteps and documenting the experience as a magazine article, a radio or TV documentary, even a book. Nothing came of it, for reasons which, to anyone who knows Kevin, don't need explaining.

   Kevin's home is a village outside Cambridge, so deep in the English countryside that it can seem like something reconstructed on the back lot of Ealing Studios circa 1948. A stream flows at the foot of the garden, the crack of willow on leather echoes from the cricket field beyond the hedge, and just up the road, a half-timbered pub serves a selection of local ales and a bar lunch of homemade beef pies.

This rural tranquility makes Kevin's other activities that much more improbable. As a busy journalist, one week might find him on the Antarctic ice, the next in a helicopter rising off the deck of an aircraft carrier in the Mediterranean. His hobbies range even further afield. Writing the definitive text on his favorite animal, the moose, took him to the Canadian north woods, while his standing as chevalier in the College of Pataphysics, that companionship of mischievous intellectuals devoted to the memory of French playwright Alfred Jarry, might find him participating in a five-day bike race for tandems or delivering a scholarly discourse on the relative melting rate of ice creams.

He also directs short films about vampires, long on blood and religious symbolism. Dinner party conversation at his table has ranged from changes in methodology within the Catholic Church to the suggestive songs of prewar music hall star George Formby, complete with a capella performances over the port and Stilton of such classics as "When I'm Cleaning Windows."

Pajamas lyin' side by side
Ladies nighties I have spied
I've often seen what goes inside
When I'm cleanin' windows.

There could be no better companion for a surrealist walk, obviously, if I could just nail him down. That was a task I put on the back burner—until the morning Paul emailed me that, after three months' work, the rebind of *Last Nights of Paris* was completed and on its way to me.

Opening the heavily wrapped parcel had an element of foreboding. Would Paul have sensed in Soupault's text the same mystery and promise as myself? The moment I peeled away the last layer of bubble wrap, I knew I would not be disappointed.

For a start, he had created a special case in which to house the book. Sometimes called a clamshell case but more correctly a Solander box, these were invented by Swedish botanist Daniel Solander while working at the British Museum, where he cataloged the natural history collection between 1763 and 1782. Custom made, Solanders signify an item too precious to be entrusted to the open shelves. Most are plain, but Paul had incised the title of the book in gold on the spine and added a spray

of gold to the upper face of the box. To do so, he would have made a metal die of his design, then impressed it into the cloth-covered board with gold leaf; a process as old as the Renaissance and so rare that only a handful of artisans could achieve it with this degree of success.

Placing my thumbs on the edge of the decorated face, I eased open the two halves of the case.

Of the original binding, nothing remained. Gleaming black calf, richly decorated in gold, now covered both boards and the spine. A nocturne of black and midnight blue, spangled with gold lamplight and stars, his transformation drew me back to the Paris of Cocteau, Prévert, Satie, and those soft, smoky surrealist nights.

Bypassing the first edition's unimaginative art deco, he had audaciously accessed the symbolist artists who inspired surrealism—Odilon Redon, Gustave Moreau, Edvard Munch. On the interior of the case itself and on the fore edges of the pages, a painted design of midnight blue evoked forests and jungles. If one stood the book, spine outward, flanked by the pictures on the interior, it created a kind of diorama in which the nature of the text was reflected and amplified in black leather, gilt, and gouache. This was craft raised to the level of art.

One of my favorite poems of the beat generation is by a lesser light of the movement, Lawrence Lipton. I first heard his *Night Song for the Sleepless* read by John Carradine on an album called *Jazz Canto* that matched poetry to jazz performances. The music chosen for Lipton's verses was "Blue Sands," by drummer Chico Hamilton. Paul's binding brought to mind the subdued rumble of Hamilton's tympani, Buddy Collette's shrill flute, and Carradine's portentous bass baritone.

> *Or have we lost that ancient cunning, you and I?*
> *Night blooming symbols rooted deep*
> *Beneath some moon-bedeviled stone.*
> *Dark knowledge that we once have known.*

This was no time for hesitation. I fired off an email to Kevin, demanding his immediate presence in Paris, under pain of excommunication from all future society. An answer came almost immediately. *Arriving Friday. Let the exquisite cadavers walk again.*

36

Magnetic Fields

If the world were a cake if the sea were black ink and if trees were all street lamps what would be left for us to drink? Mr. Mirror the old-clothes man dies yesterday night in Paris it is night it is dark it's a dark night in Paris I buy a gun so much the better I kill a bystander so much the better I sell my gun Thank you Philippe Soupault in his bed born Monday baptized Tuesday married Wednesday sick Thursday dying Friday dead Saturday buried Sunday that's the life of Philippe Soupault.

PHILIPPE SOUPAULT, Littérature #19, May 1921

Kevin is not someone you forget in a hurry. Well over six feet and bulky with it, he exudes the relaxed and self-assured amiability of the animal that inspired his nickname, "Moose," as well as that beast's sense of contained force. I'd never seen him angry, nor did I know anyone who had, but it wasn't something we were in a hurry to witness.

So far I'd withheld from him the information that what suggested him as a collaborator was a passage from *Last Nights of Paris*. As the narrator passes the Gare d'Orsay, still then a railway station and not the art museum it became, he's startled to hear someone blundering up the steps from the underground concourse—a sailor, carrying a cylindrical kit bag of white canvas.

> *He approached me, stumbling, and raising his free hand to his beret, asked me, "Paris?"*
>
> *He had an enormous head, red, blond, the face of a strangler, with thin lips and enormous brown hands.*
>
> *"This is Paris."*
>
> *"Thanks." And stumbling, stumbling, he moved off.*

How would Kevin feel about such a comparison? Particularly since, as was later revealed, the sailor's bag was filled with . . . well, never mind. I decided to leave it until we could discuss it face-to-face.

The rest of the week gave me time to reread *Last Nights*. It left me even more convinced. No book conveyed so effectively those qualities that distinguished the Paris night from that of London or Berlin or New York. At the same time, I had even less idea of how to adapt its events into the material for a walk.

The story begins innocently enough. Soupault's nameless narrator, lingering in a café in the early evening, avoiding the steady soaking rain, catches the eye of a girl—a prostitute, he assumes, since, in those days, women sitting alone in cafés generally were.

She says her name is Georgette. They leave together, wandering through the streets around the Luxembourg Gardens, then down to the Seine. From time to time, men approach Georgette, who accompanies them into an *hôtel de passe* while the narrator waits. When she emerges, they resume their promenade.

Arriving at the Seine and the Pont des Arts, the bridge leading from the esplanade of the Institut de France to the Louvre, they encounter the sailor again, with his bulging white bag, but joined now by a parade of sinister creatures, criminals, or worse. Thereafter, the narrator, Georgette, her criminal companions, and a friendly black dog wander around a city that increasingly reflects the disjointed continuity of a dream.

The night clung to the trees, then, lying in wait in
the shadowy spaces or crouching in the long, narrow

*and somber streets, it seemed to spy upon us as if
we were emerging from some dive. The least noise
was a catastrophe, the least breath a great terror.
We walked in the eternal mud. Step by step we sank
into the thickness of night, lost as if forever.*

Choosing a poet rather than a novelist to translate the book had been an inspiration. In the hands of
William Carlos Williams, both the city and the night
become characters in the story. In *The Love Song of J.
Alfred Prufrock,* written almost a decade before, T. S.
Eliot humanized London as "a patient etherized upon a
table" and wrote of "streets that follow like a tedious argument / Of insidious intent." Williams also saw Paris
as a person, but not anaesthetized. Towering and malevolent, he looms over the city like Fantômas.

But how could this be the blueprint for a walk?
With the novelist's freedom to improvise, Soupault only
hinted at some locations. Others that he described in
detail were kilometers apart. Some no longer existed.
The old Palais du Trocadéro, for example, built for
the International Exposition of 1878, was demolished
in 1935 to make way for the handsome art deco Palais
de Chaillot. The deepest of its cellars still housed an
aquarium, but not the echoing cavern of Soupault's de-

scription, in which conspirators whisper, surrounded by "great squares of luminous water where long fish floated half asleep."

The phone rang. "Just got off the Eurostar," said Kevin. "Be with you in half an hour."

I put down the phone with a sense of the curtain about to go up. Soon I'd hear the three thumps of a staff on the boards of the stage that traditionally warned a performance was about to begin.

37

The Hotel of Great Men

I'll take as my departure point L'Hôtel des Grands Hommes.

PHILIPPE SOUPAULT

N ice night for it," said Kevin, wiping water from his eyebrows.

True to Soupault, a light rain had begun falling over the city almost as soon as Kevin arrived. We stayed in the apartment until midnight, occasionally taking a break from drinking and talking to stick our heads out-side, but when midnight arrived with no relief in sight, I suggested we set off.

Just after 1:00 a.m., we reached the top of rue Soufflot.

Sifting down, the rain conferred halos on the street lamps around Place du Panthéon, painting a gleam on its cobbles, varnishing the gray steel roofs. Ahead of us, dominating everything, towered the Panthéon, a secular cathedral and France's temple of top people. Inside, under the dome, ticking tirelessly in the dark, in tune with the rotation of the planet, a sixty-pound lead weight sheathed in brass swung at the end of a wire 220 feet long—Foucault's pendulum, proving in stately progress something the French knew instinctively anyway, that Paris is the center of the earth.

Above the colonnade outside, an inscription announced *Aux grands hommes la patrie reconnaissante*—To great men, the nation's gratitude. Beneath the marble floor, a crypt held the bones of those men and women found worthy of France's highest honor. Dylan Thomas wrote, "After the first death, there is no other." How like the French to confute him, digging up the remains of the famous, and, once their importance in the national narrative was established, giving them a second burial by re-interring them here—just as working stonemasons had re-interred the skeletons of the unknown in the catacombs. An identical impulse—but, as in all real estate, location was everything.

In September 1918, twenty-two-year-old André Breton finished his military service as a medical aide and enrolled to study medicine. To be near the Val-de-Grâce hospital, he took a room in the Hôtel des Grands Hommes, a then-down-at-heel establishment facing the Panthéon. Over the next six months, he was visited by Paul Éluard, Louis Aragon, and Philippe Soupault, all Dadaists who shared his impatience with the movement. In 1922, they would instigate an explosive break that led to the birth of surrealism.

Soupault, only twenty-one, edited a thin yellow-covered journal called, tersely, *Littérature*. In the spring of 1919, to test Breton's concept of "automatic writing," the two met at the hotel and spent eight consecutive days experimenting with the technique. Breton explained the process in his *First Manifesto of Surrealism*.

> *Put yourself in the most passive, or receptive, state you can. Write swiftly with no preconceived subject, swiftly enough that you cannot retain it, and are not tempted to re-read. The first sentence will arise spontaneously, it being the case in truth that each second there is a sentence, unknown to our conscious thought, which only asks to be externalized.*

Soupault recalled:

We wrote, side by side, in all good faith, those pages
which would provoke what André Breton called,
proudly, the surrealist revolution. We were surprised,
in my case stupefied, when we reread what we had
written. Sometimes we burst into laughter. And I
will never forget the laughter of Breton, something
between that of a baby and a rooster.

When the experiments appeared in *Littérature* as
"Les Champs Magnétiques," neither Soupault nor
Breton apologized for the fact that it had all been fun.
Was that why no surrealist has ever been elevated to the
Panthéon? To the French, literature should be no laugh-
ing matter.

Even though it now had three stars, the Hôtel des
Grands Hommes remained a respectful distance from
the building that justified its name. Crossing the square,
we read the marble plaque set into the wall by the main
entrance.

Dans cet hôtel au cours du printemps 1919 André **BRETON** & Philippe
SOUPAULT ont inventé l'écriture automatique et donné naissance au
surréalisme en écrivant "**Les champs magnétiques.**"

Kevin Jackson

It was a stretch to claim the writing of "Les Champs Magnétiques" "gave birth to surrealism." That didn't happen officially until 1922, when the Dadaists put Breton "on trial"—naturally in a café, the Closerie des Lilas. The brawl that followed decisively launched the new movement, trampling Tzara's playful experiment in the process. But we were clearly in surrealist country. With Soupault as guide, how could it be otherwise?

Kevin took the obligatory snapshot of me grinning next to the plaque.

"What now?"

I turned to face back down rue Soufflot, toward the Luxembourg Gardens, now locked and dark. We both sensed that the night was another country. They did things differently here, and the prudent visitor conducted himself with caution and circumspection.

I pulled my scarf more snugly around my neck.

"We walk."

38

The Hour of Crimes

*Everything tends to make us believe that there
exists a certain point of the mind at which life and
death, the real and the imagined, past and future,
the communicable and the incommunicable, high
and low, cease to be perceived as contradictions.*

ANDRÉ BRETON

On such a night, with few people out, Paris becomes a city of shop windows. Reticent by day,
they retreat from our attention into the shadows. At
night, however, lit from within, they reach out to invite
us, opening like flowers. *Night blooming simples, rooted
deep* . . . At such times, the traffic between seller and
client turns sensual. The French don't speak of "window
shopping" but of *lèche-vitrine*—window licking.

Keeping out of the rain brought us closer to the windows of shops at which, under normal conditions, we'd never have paused. One vaguely described "gift shop" offered porcelain rabbits and small white jars decorated with a finial in the form of a pink skull. For what function? Neither of us could imagine.

I recognized one nineteenth-century façade of green-painted wood, since it had been in the news. Though the name read Pharmacie Lhopitallier, the Lhopitallier family who did business here for more than a century had recently sold out. The interior, with its paneling and banks of wooden cupboards, was now preserved in the Musée Carnavalet. Its antique façade remained, but as the new owners were free to sell whatever they liked, the windows that had once been filled with antique pill bottles and ads for patent medicines now displayed, incongruously, mannequins draped with dresses in *un style bohème et chic*.

At the foot of rue Soufflot, on the usually busy boulevard Saint-Michel, nothing stirred. The junction with rue de Médicis, normally one of the busiest in Paris, was deserted. No pedestrians interrupted the emptiness of its streets under the rain. Naturally the surrealists felt an affinity with the night. Paris after dark, drained of people, became a blank page on which they would exercise their imagination.

If the ruling minds of this walk were Soupault and Breton, the eye was that of Giorgio de Chirico, master of the empty plaza, the deserted colonnade. As we sheltered in the arcade at the rear of the Théàtre de l'Odéon, with the barred darkness of the Luxembourg Gardens opposite, across rue de Médicis, Kevin said, "Wasn't there something in the book about sadistic bachelors . . . ?"

I dug out my dog-eared paperback and found the passage.

" 'The rue de Medicis along which we were strolling at a fair pace is sad around ten-thirty at night . . .' "

I looked around the drafty colonnade. *True enough.*

I went on. " 'It is a street of everlasting rain . . .' "

The drizzle continued to drift down through the lights. *He got that right as well.*

" 'It is said,' " I continued, " 'that along one side of it is the meeting place of masochistic bachelors. A modest and silent club. Here umbrellas take on the appearance of a flock.' "

So this had been what was generally called a "meat rack" where seekers for the more painful sensations came to shop. Similar places existed in most cities, often under colonnades such as this. Sadomasochism is a diversion as specialized as stamp collecting. One might wait hours to find a partner of matching tastes. Shelter was desirable. So was an umbrella, not to mention a raincoat, even if one wore nothing under it.

"This is getting a little creepy," Kevin said. "Next thing, we'll run into Georgette."

"For that, we'd need a café."

We moved out of shelter and turned into rue Tournon, but even Café Tournon was shut. Some aspects of the Paris night might survive from Soupault's time, but since waiters were now unionized, few had to work past midnight.

"I'd settle for the dog," I said, pulling my head deeper into my collar.

Kevin coughed. "Don't look now . . ."

About a hundred meters ahead of us, a square black van had just parked. A woman got out. Following her was a black dog.

"Did I say a bit creepy?" Kevin said. "Let me revise that. This is *extremely* creepy."

The woman watched warily as we walked toward her. The dog, less suspicious, sniffed and, scenting no fear or menace, nuzzled my leg. From inside the van, a man looked out.

"Bon soir." I held up the pocket recorder with which I'd been taking notes. "We're making a radio documentary for the BBC."

It wasn't too much of a lie. Both of us had worked for the BBC, and we might conceivably turn this into a program one day.

"Are you French?" I asked.

"No. Dutch," the man said in English. "Are we okay to park here?"

I looked around at the empty street. "I don't see why not."

From a glimpse of the interior, their van had been adapted into a mobile bedroom, with bunk beds.

"Are you going to sleep here?"

The woman said, "We were out in the suburbs, but it is not so nice there. You won't tell?"

"Our lips are sealed," Kevin said. "Your name isn't Georgette, I suppose?"

She frowned. "No. Eva." She waved toward her friend, who was making up the beds. "And this is Paul. You are looking for a Georgette?"

"Not really," I said. "It's a long story."

Ten minutes later, Kevin and I drank cold beer in the only café on rue de Buci that remained open.

"A strange night," he said.

"They're all strange."

He shook his head. "That woman . . . and the dog . . ."

It had been an interesting coincidence—if one believed in coincidences. What if we had lingered on the empty street, perhaps stepped into the interior of that van . . . ? An infinite universe of possibilities opened before me. I blinked it closed. *Don't go there!*

"What now?" Kevin said, looking out at the rain, now heavier. "Want to go on?"

"I don't think so."

He nodded sympathetically. I didn't explain that it

wasn't the rain that dissuaded me. Following Soupault's ramblings had made me see a more fundamental problem with walking by night. Paris by day, a working city, was in the business of being accessible. Bakers sold the same breads. Restaurants offered their set menus. The works of Picasso and Delacroix were reliably on show in galleries and museums.

At night, however, those rules no longer applied. "Paris by Night" tours stuck to the Moulin Rouge and Folies Bergère because they were safe—not from mug-

gers and pickpockets but from ideas. To set out into the night, clothed in nothing but innocence, was to invite the invasion of everything that this city represented; the satisfaction of desire, the embrace of change, even the will to destruction; the face of *l'inconnue* was proof that the waters of the Seine ran dark and fast.

Was this the truth the sixth tapestry in the Cluny meant to convey? Might its motto, *À Mon Seul Désir*, also mean "by my will alone"? With her magic unicorn and her omnicompetent maid, the lady of the tapestries controlled her world. She had merely to express a desire for it to be realized. But formulating that desire and framing the request took imagination. To gratify the five senses, one needed a sixth. And that, as the surrealists understood, rested with each of us alone.

In my capacity as guide, I could help with the first five senses. But after that, each of us had to make our own voyage of exploration. That was the message of both *Last Nights of Paris* and *Midnight in Paris*. We must create our own *griffe*—our secret park, that fugitive scent, our own Georgette.

So in answer to the lady from Montreal—no, I don't do night walks. Each of us must, in our own way, as with a new lover, seduce, or allow ourselves to be seduced by the Paris night.

But I can unlock the gate that leads into the dark, push it slightly ajar . . .

Allez-y, mes amis. Paris and its nights are yours.

❈ · ACKNOWLEDGMENTS · ❈

There is no room to list all the people who contributed to this book, but foremost among them must be the many visitors from around the world whom it has been my pleasure to lead on literary walks. Their comments and insights have caused me to look at my adoptive city in a new light, and I'm profoundly grateful.

Among those friends who lent their shoulder to this particular wheel, my warmest thanks to Milou de Castellane, Kate McLean, Paul Delrue, Terrance Gelenter, Kevin Jackson, Kristi Anderson, Christopher Jones, Annick Joueo-Launay, and Kristin Duncombe.

As always, Peter Hubbard, my editor at Harper Perennial, was an insightful collaborator, as were Nick Amphlett and the whole Harper production team. Thanks also to Jonathan Lloyd at Curtis Brown. *Perfer et obdura; dolor hic tibi proderit olim.*

✳ · PHOTO CREDITS · ✳

Page 14. *What's New Pussycat*. Famous Artists Productions/United Artists.

Page 74. *Paris Nous Appartient*. Ajym Films/Les Films du Carrosse /Merlyn Films.

Page 111. *Murder at the Vanities*. Paramount Pictures/Universal Studios Home Entertainment.

Page 123. *The Merry Widow*. Metro-Goldwyn-Mayer.

Page 210. *Algiers*. Walter Wanger Productions/United Artists.

Page 291. *Les Jeux Sont Faits*. Les Films Gibé/Lopert Pictures Corporation.

Other photographs by Louise Baxter, Jacques Henric, Brassaï, Flavia Broï, Marie-Dominique Montel, and the author.

acte gratuite, 273–274, 284
adult film, 190–194
Aérosol, Jef, 170
African Americans, 42–43, 67–68, 119
Alexandria Quartet, The (L. Durrell), 256
Algiers (film), 53, 209, 210, 215–216
Algren, Nelson, 181
Allen, Woody, 9–16, 198–199
Ambassadors, The (James), 5
American in Paris, An (film), 45, 163, 258
American in Paris, An (Gershwin), 55
Les Amuse-Gueules, 66–67
Angelina, 177–179
les années folles, 6–8, 10–11, 41–44
Aragon, Louis, 228, 243–244, 266, 270, 310
Arc de Triomphe, 112, 170, 262
Arden, Elizabeth, 225
Arletty, 52
Armstrong, Louis, 12
Arp, Hans, 271
Arsan, Emmanuelle, 182
Art Press (journal), 185
L'As du Fallafel, 174–175
Ashley, April (George Jamieson), 43–44
d'Aubusson, Pierre, 36
Au Chai de l'Abbaye (café), 33, 56–61
Au Petit Versailles, 177–178
Auschwitz, 172
automatic writing, 277–278, 310–312

Babette's Feast (Dinesen), 112–113
Baker, Chet, 65
Baker, Josephine, 12
Bakewell, Jean, 70
Balanchine, Georges, 198, 202
Baldwin, James, 42
Balladur, Édouard, 126
balm of Gilead, 237
Balzac, Honoré de, 132, 148
Barbarella (film), 201
Barnes, Djuna, 10, 283
Beach, Sylvia, 8
"beards," 195
beat generation, 301
Beaubourg (café), 40–41
Bechet, Sidney, 12–13
Beecher, Henry Ward, 279
beer gardens *(guinguettes)*, 211
beeswax, 238–239
beggars, 212–213, 217–219
Belladonna, Angelina, 177–179
belle époque, 48, 178
Benjamin, Walter, 54, 185–187
Bennett, Alan, 237
Bentley, Toni, 202–203
Benton, Oscar, 202
Berkeley, Ron, 16
Bernardin, Alain, 199–200, 202–203
Bernardini, Micheline, 199–200
Berry, Walter, 7
Big Heat, The (film), 130
bikini swimsuit, 199–200

birdsong, 211–212
Birkin, Jane, 182
Bizet, Georges, 37
Black Sun Press, 261–262
Bloom Where You Are Planted, 188, 194
Bois de Boulogne, 183, 184, 262
bookbinding, 279–284, 299–301
Boulez, Pierre, 41
Bourgois, 224
Boyer, Charles, 136, 210, 215
Boyle, Kay, 7
Brady, Pam, 154
Brassaï, 134, 259–265, 266
Brassens, George, 167
Brasserie Lipp, 290
Brasserie Vagenende, 101
bread, 154–164
Breton, André, 72, 217, 257, 270–274, 277–278, 310–312, 314, 316
Brillat-Savarin, Jean Anthelme, 83
Brisson, Carl, 120
brothels, 93–95, 122–125, 135, 174
Browning, Robert, 25
Buñuel, Luis, 10, 156
burglary, 51
Burton, Richard, 16
butchers, 30, 31–32

Café des Amateurs, 134
Café du Rendez-Vous, 42, 285–286, 291–296
cafés, 12, 30–31, 33, 39–52, 134, 161–164, 177–178, 180, 234. *See also specific cafés*
  lavatories, 100–101
  as uteruses, 285–286, 292–296
  waiters, 294–296, 317
  writers in, 39–44
Callaghan, Morley, 7
Callaway, Jesse Joe, 56–61

Canute, King, 88
capital punishment, 103–109, 115
Carmen (opera), 37, 112
Carné, Marcel, 168–169
Caron, Leslie, 258
Carradine, John, 301
Carrière, Jean-Claude, 94–95, 156
Carroll, Lewis, 103
Casino de Paris, 199–200
Castle, Vernon and Irene, 67
catacombs/tunnels, 286–291, 292, 309
Cather, Willa, 72
Céline, Louis-Ferdinand, 136
cemeteries, 211, 212
Le Chabanäis (brothel), 93–94, 174
Champs-Élysées, 12, 94
Les Champs Magnétiques–The Magnetic Fields, 277–278, 310–312
Chandler, Raymond, 18
Chanel, Coco, 220, 224
Charles Stuart (Bonnie Prince Charlie), 131
Chevalier, Maurice, 123
Chez Marianne, 175–176
Chirac, Jacques, 126
Chirico, Giorgio de, 316
Citroën, André, 234
Closerie des Lilas (café), 41, 312–313
Club Saint-Germain, 66
Cluny abbey, 35–38, 321–322
Cocteau, Jean, 11, 168–169, 190
Colbert, Claudette, 136
Colette, 113
Collette, Buddy, 301
Collins, Wilkie, 282
Coltrane, John, 70
Commune (1871), 31, 231–233
Communist Party, 272
Congreve, William, 188
Connolly, Cyril, 70

Conover, Will, 66
Contact Editions, 8
Contrescarpe, 134–138, 147, 150
Convent des Augustins, 125
convulsionists, 132–134
Le Corbusier, 169
Corday, Charlotte, 108
Coty, François, 224
La Coupole (café), 30, 42, 57, 101
courtesans, 124
Coward, Noel, 121
Crabbe, Larry "Buster," 137
Crazy Horse Saloon, 15, 196, 197–203
Crèmerie Polidor, 11
créperie, 88–91
Crevel, René, 271
croque monsieur, 157–164
Crosby, Caresse, 184, 261–263
Crosby, Harry, 7, 184, 261–262
Curzon, Lord, 48

Dadaism, 310–312
Dalí, Salvador, 10, 93–94, 183, 198, 202, 271
Davies, Marion, 23–24
Davis, George, 7
Davis, Miles, 66, 70
Death of a Salesman (A. Miller), 121
de Beauvoir, Simone, 70, 181
Debord, Guy, 247
Debussy, Claude, 262
decapitation, 103–109
Decouflé, Philippe, 200–202
defecation, 95–102, 132, 134
de Gaulle, Charles, 169
Dekobra, Maurice, 197
Delanoë, Bertrand, 50–51
de La Pérouse, Jean-Françoise, 115
Delon, Alain, 191
Delrue, Paul, 279–284
de Molay, Jacques, 247

Deneuve, Catherine, 191
Depression, 136, 143
Le Deserteur (Vian), 162–163
Desnos, Robert, 275–277
deuxième (number 2) subway line, 209–212, 215–219
Deux Magots (café), 42, 229, 274–275, 290
Deval, Jacques, 135–138
Dickens, Charles, 282
Dinesen, Isak, 112–113
Dior, Christian, 41–42
Dita von Teese, 202–203
dogs, 40–41, 96, 98, 318–319
La Dolce Vita (film), 17
Dombasle, Arielle, 202
Dôme (café), 30–31, 42
Donner, Clive, 15
Don't Drink the Water (Allen), 13
Doolittle, Hilda, 7
Dream of a Rarebit Fiend, The (McCay), 158
Dr. Jekyll and Mr. Hyde (Stevenson), 29
Drosso's, 261–264
drugs, 43, 119, 121, 124, 260, 261–264
Dublin, 22, 24, 283
Duchamp, Marcel, 277
Dullin, Charles, 291
Durrell, Gerald, 255–256
Durrell, Lawrence, 256

Église Saint-Sulpice, 95
Eiffel Tower, 112, 170, 204
Ekberg, Anita, 17
Eliot, T. S., 91, 217, 245–246, 306
Ellington, Duke, 119
Éluard, Gala, 182–183
Éluard, Paul, 182, 271, 283, 310
Emmanuelle (film), 182, 185
Les Enfants du Paradis (film), 52
Ernst, Max, 182, 271

Index

Escoffier, Auguste, 159
Europe, James Reese, 67–68
Everyone Says I Love You (film), 16
excrement, 95–102, 132, 134
exhibitionism, 180, 181
existentialism, 41–44, 66–67
Exquisite Corpses (game), 273, 277
Exterminating Angel, The (film), 10

Fantômas, 74, 275–277, 306
feasts, 76–77, 112–114, 144–145
Festival of Saint-Denis, 200
Feuillade, Louis, 275–277
film clubs, 196
film noir, 270
firing squads, 106
fish markets, 31–32, 84–85
Fitzgerald, F. Scott, 7, 9, 10–11
Fitzgerald, Zelda, 10
Flanner, Janet, 224, 274–275
Flash Gordon serials, 119
flea markets, 81–82
Fleurus (café), 42, 161–164
Flore (café), 42, 47, 290
Folies Bergère, 197, 320–321
Fonda, Jane, 181
fondue, 159
Fonssagrives, Mia, 15
food markets, 30–33, 84–85, 147–148
Formby, George, 298–299
Fouras (Paris on Sea), 78–92
Fragonard, 228–229
French Revolution (1789), 28,
    104–105, 157

Gabin, Jean, 143
Gainsbourg, Serge, 182
Gallant, Mavis, 39–40, 41, 55–56, 87
gardens, 226–227, 240–251. *See also*
    specific parks and gardens
Gare d'Orsay, 304

Gare du Nord, 214
gay culture, 169, 171–172, 196–197,
    260, 272
Gelenter, Terrance, 45–52, 53, 61
Genet, Jean, 40–41
gentrification, 169
George Cinq, 203–205
Gershwin, George, 55, 121, 204
Girodias, Maurice, 42
Godard, Jean-Luc, 214
Goddard, Jacqueline, 30–31
Goodsir, Agnes, 7
graffiti taggers, 288
Grahame, Kenneth, 250–251
Grappelli, Stéphane, 44, 69
graveyards, 211, 212, 286–291, 292
Great Gatsby, The (Fitzgerald), 195
Greco, Juliette, 44
Greece, 141–143, 145
Greene, Graham, 18, 250, 280
la griffe, 32–33, 35–36
group sex, 182–187, 262
grunion running, 24–25
Guerlain, Jacques, 221–225
Le Guide Culinaire (Escoffier), 159
Guide Porcelaine to the Loos of Paris
    (Routh), 100, 101
Guide to the Literary Pilgrimage
    (Thurber), 265
guillotine, 103–109, 115
Guillotin, J. M. V., 106
Guillotin, Joseph-Ignace, 103–106
Guimard, Hector, 212
Guinness, Alec, 47, 237
Gypsies, 68–69, 124–125

Halász, Gyula (Brassaï), 134, 259–265,
    266
Les Halles, 30, 31
Hamilton, Chico, 301
Hammett, Dashiell, 282

Hamsun, Knut, 149
hanging, 104, 108–109
Hart, Kitty Carlisle, 110–112, 115–121
Hart, Larry, 55
Hart, Moss, 110, 116, 117
Haussmann, Georges Eugène, Baron, 29–30, 31, 168, 169, 231, 244, 286–287
Hearst, William Randolph, 23–24
Heart-Ons, 190
Hemingway, Ernest, 7, 8, 10, 11, 41, 44, 129, 134, 148, 250, 257–259
Henric, Jacques, 185–187
Henry IV, 167, 246–247
Henry VIII, 96–97
Heptaméron (Marguerite de Navarre), 193
L'Heure Bleue (perfume), 222–224
Hiller, Wendy, 129–130
Himes, Chester, 42, 43
Histoire d'O (film), 182, 185
Hitler, Adolf, 68
homeless population, 220
homosexuality, 169, 171–172, 196–197, 260, 272
horses, 97–99
Hôtel des Grands Hommes, 310–313
Hôtel des Invalides, 94
Hôtel de Ville, 51
Hôtel George V, 12
Hôtel Grand, 124
Hôtel La Louisiane, 70–71
hôtels de passe, 30, 135, 305
Hugo, Victor, 132
Huis Clos (Sartre), 288–289
hunger, 147–150
Hunger (Hamsun), 149
Hydra (Greek island), 141–143, 145

I Know Where I'm Going (film), 129–130

Île de la Cité, 72, 73, 246–251
L'Inconnue de la Seine (unknown girl of the Seine), 247–249, 321
Ingrid, 285–287, 292–296
Institut de France, 305
l'Institute de Recherche et Coordination Acoustique/ Musique (IRCAM), 40–41
International Exposition of 1878, 306
It Was a Navy Boy (Owen), 1

Jackson, Kevin, 297, 307–319
James, Henry, 5
Jamieson, George (April Ashley), 43–44
jams, 79–80
Japanese *chikan densha* ("pervert train"), 214–215
Jarry, Alfred, 298
jazz, 12–13, 42, 44, 65–71, 268–269, 275
Jazz Canto (album), 301
Je T'aime Moi Non Plus (film), 182
Les Jeux Sont Faits–The Chips Are Down (Sartre), 288–291
Jews, 68, 113, 168, 171–173
Joe Goldenberg's, 172–173
Johnson, Lyndon, 126
jonchée, 85–86
Joyce, James, 8, 22, 134, 189
Juta, Jan, 280

Kate, 230–239
Kelly, Gene, 163, 258
Kelly, Ned, 90
Kern, Jerome, 46, 121
Kevin, 297, 307–319
King's Evil, 167–168
Knights Templar, 247
Kohner, Frederick, 222

Lacan, Jacques, 156

Lady and the Unicorn tapestries, 36–38, 321–322

Lady of the Night (night-blooming jasmine), 226–227

Laerdal, Asmund, 249

Lalique, René, 224

Lamarr, Hedy, 53, 210, 215–216

Lambert, Dave, 26

Lampedusa, Giuseppe di, 114

Lang, Fritz, 130

La Rochefoucauld, François de, 98, 156

Lasser, Louise, 16

Last Nights of Paris, The (Soupault), 267–268, 270, 283–284, 285, 292, 299–301, 303–307, 322

Laurencin, Marie, 245–246

lavatories, 80–81, 95–102

Lawrence, D. H., 279–281

Lawrence of Arabia (film), 20

Lawrence, T. E., 20

le Carré, John, 135

Le Gallienne, Richard, 248–249

Légendes de Catherine M. (Henric), 185

Lehár, Franz, 123

Lempicka, Tamara de, 214

Lenin, Vladimir, 7

Leopard, The (Lampedusa), 114

lesbianism, 245–246

Levant, Oscar, 45

Lévy, Bernard-Henri, 202

Lipton, Lawrence, 301

Littérature (journal), 310, 311

Livesey, Roger, 130

Llewellyn, Richard, 282

Logue, Christopher, 42

Loh, Sandra Tsing, 25

London, 2, 3, 22, 24

Louis XIV, 127–128

Louis XV, 133, 167–168, 221

Louis XVI, 115, 157

Louvre, 22–23, 28, 34, 305

Love Song of J. Alfred Prufrock, The (Eliot), 306

Loy, Mina, 7

Luter, Claude, 13

Luxembourg Gardens, 41, 42, 74, 99, 148, 161–162, 243–245, 260, 305, 313, 316

Machiavelli, Niccolo, 22

Mackay, Helen, 238

maitre d', 125–128

Maîtresse (film), 196

Malraux, André, 169

Man Ray, 30–31, 271

Marais, 168–176, 189

Marat, Jean-Paul, 108

Marguerite de Navarre, 193

marijuana, 119, 121

Marx Brothers, 116

Marx, Groucho, 122

Mary, Queen of Scots, 131

Maxim's, 122–124

McAlmon, Robert, 6

McCay, Winsor, 158

McDonald's, 161

McLaren, Malcolm, 285

McMurtry, Larry, 35

Le Meilleure Boulangerie de France (TV program), 155–156

Melly, George, 268–269, 277

Mérimée, Prosper, 37

Merry Widow, The (operetta), 123–124

Mesens, Édouard, 182, 268

Mesens, Sybil, 182

métro (subway), 209–219

Michael, Gertrude, 119

Middleton, Charles, 119

Midnight in Paris (film), 9–13, 16, 322

Miller, Arthur, 121

Miller, Henry, 42, 95, 99, 101, 195, 245–246, 255, 259–260
Millet, Catherine, 184–187
Milou, 197–205
mime, 218–219
Minotaure (magazine), 257
Les Misérables (Hugo), 132, 204
Molnár, Ferenc, 180–181
Monk, Thelonious, 66–67
Monroe, Marilyn, 110
"Monsieur de Paris," 108–109
Montand, Yves, 163
Montmartre, 73–74, 210–212, 230–239, 270
Montparnasse, 6, 30–31, 42, 55, 57, 95, 188, 222, 270
Moreau, Gustave, 301
morphine, 124
Mouffetard, 131–138, 147
Moulin Rouge, 9, 197, 320–321
"moveable feast," 7, 257–259
Munch, Edvard, 301
Murder at the Vanities (film), 111, 117, 118, 119–121
Musée Carnavalet, 316
Musée de la Chasse et de la Nature, 174
Musée National du Moyen Age, 35–38
Museum of Eroticism, 9
mushroom growing, 288
music, 55–61, 65–71, 212–213. *See also* jazz
Musidora, 275
My Family and Other Animals (G. Durrell), 255–256

Nadja (Breton), 270
Napoleon I (Napoleon Bonaparte), 130–131, 234, 244
Napoleon III, 97, 231, 244
Native Son (Wright), 43
Nazis, 68, 185, 289

New York Café, 180
New York City, 2, 3, 14–15, 22, 23, 55–56
New York City Ballet, 202
New Yorker, The, 274–275
Nietzsche, Friedrich, 34, 65
Night at the Opera, A (film), 116
Nightmare Alley (film), 289
Night Song for the Sleepless (Lipton), 301
night walks, 33, 34, 45–52
   five senses in, 32, 36–38, 53–61, 283, 321–322
   nuit blanche, 50–52
   potential drawbacks of, 51–52, 53
Nolan, Sidney, 90
Notre Dame, 74
Nouvelle cuisine, 161
nuit blanche, 50–52

Olympia Press, 42
Opéra, 101–102, 124, 244
Opera Ball, The (operetta), 123
opium, 261–264
Orangerie, 245
orgies, 182–187, 262
Orphée (film), 168–169
Orwell, George, 134–135, 149–150
O'Toole, Peter, 11–14, 198
Owen, Wilfred, 1

Pagliero, Marcello, 291
Paine, Tom, 7–8
Palais de Chaillot, 306–307
Palais du Trocadéro, 306
Palin, Michael, 147
panhandlers, 212–213, 217–219
Panthéon, 309–310
paraffin wax, 237–239
Parc des Buttes-Chaumont, 243–244
Paris (musical), 7

Pâris, François de, 132

Les Paris Gourmandes, 173, 175–176

Paris La Nuit (Brassaï), 260–265, 266

Paris Nous Appartient–Paris Belongs to Us (Rivette), 74

Paris Peasant (Aragon), 266, 270

Paris Writers' Workshop, 5–7

Parker, Charlie "Bird," 66, 70

Parker, Dorothy, 23–24

parks, public, 243–251. *See also specific public parks and gardens*

Parsons, E. Bryham, 295–296

les partouzeurs, 182–187, 262

Paul, Elliot, 7

Le Père Goriot (Balzac), 132, 148

Père Lachaise cemetery, 212

perfume, 25, 172, 220–229

Périer, François, 52

peripatetic monks, 26–28

La Pérouse (restaurant), 115–121, 122, 124, 125, 127

Perroy, Jean-François, 170

Peter, Paul and Mary, 163

Pharmacie Lhopitallier, 315–316

photography, 259–265

Picasso, Pablo, 7

pickpocketing, 51

Pierrepoint, Albert, 109

Pigalle, 9, 53, 94–95

Pink Panther, The (film), 13

pissoirs, 98–102

Place Blanche, 216–217, 271–272

Place Dauphine, Île de la Cité, 72, 73, 246–251

Place de Clichy, 218

Place de Furstenberg, 245–246

Place de la Nation, 213

Place du Tertre, 230–236

Playboy, 182, 190, 198–199

ploughman's lunch, 158

Le Pluriel (club), 178–180

Poilane, Lionel, 160

Pompidou Center, 40, 170

Pont Alexandre III, 94

"poor food," 113–114, 141–146

pop culture, 275

pornographic film, 190–194

Porte Dauphine, 184–185, 213, 262

Porter, Cole, 7, 10–11, 46, 183, 204

Les Portes de la Nuit (film), 168–169

Powell, Bud, 12–13

Powell, Michael, 129–130

Power, Tyrone, 289

Prentiss, Paula, 15

Presle, Micheline, 291

Prévert, Jacques, 141, 177, 249–250

privies, 98–99

Procope (café), 30

prostitution, 30, 101, 135, 187, 205, 214, 260, 293–294, 305

psychogeography, 247

Quiet Days in Clichy (H. Miller), 42, 195, 260, 266

raclette, 159

radio, 65–66, 118

Réage, Pauline, 182

Redon, Odilon, 301

Reinhardt, Django, 68–69

Rendezvous (café), 42, 285–286, 291–296

restaurants, 88–91, 115–128, 150–151, 172–173, 174–176, 234, 295–296

Resusci Anne, 249

Richard II (Shakespeare), 2

Ritchie, Lionel, 204

Ritz Bar, 30

Rivette, Jacques, 74

Robbe-Grillet, Alain, 156

Roberts, Julia, 16

Rotonde (café), 30

Round Midnight (film), 70–71
Rousseau, Henri, 90
Routh, Jonathan, 100, 101
Rowley, Hazel, 42–43
Rowling, J. K., 39
Ruskin, John, 56

Sacré-Coeur, 73–74, 233, 234–239
sadomasochism, 182, 196, 317
Saint Denis, 27–28
Saint-Étienne-du-Mont, 11
Saint-Germain-des-Prés, 42–44,
    55, 68
Saint-Médard, 132–134
Saint-Sulpice, 100
salade composée, 151–152
salades gourmandes, 152–153
Sanchez, Tania, 225
Sand, Georges, 36–37
Sandy, 188–194
Sanson, Henri-Clément, 109
Sartre, Jean-Paul, 41, 66, 70, 168–169,
    288–289
Schmidt, Tobias, 105–106
Schroeder, Barbet, 196
Schulz-Köhn, Dietrich, 68
Schwitters, Kurt, 269
scrofula, 167–168
Sea and Sardinia (D. H. Lawrence),
    279–281
séance, 268, 271–272
Seaver, Richard, 42
Sellers, Peter, 11–14
sex clubs, 178–180
Shakespeare & Company, 8, 283
Shakespeare, William, 2, 47, 93
Sherwood, Robert E., 136
shoplifting, 4
Signoret, Simone, 47, 163
Simon Says (game), 271
Smiley's People (le Carré), 135

smoking, 162, 178, 179
soaps, 81
Solander, Daniel, 299
Sorbonne, 47, 112, 256–257
Soupault, Philippe, 70, 267–268, 270,
    272, 277–278, 283–284, 285, 292,
    299–301, 303–310, 316, 317, 320
sourdough bread, 160
Le Sphinx (brothel), 95
Stardust Memories (film), 13
Stark, Freya, 267
Stearns, Harold, 7
Stein, Gertrude, 10, 11, 57, 148, 162
Stevenson, Robert Louis, 28–29
Stow, Randolph, 91
Strauss-Kahn, Dominique, 187
street artists, 234
street surfaces, 53, 96–97, 211, 260
street vendors, 31–33, 148
strip clubs, 15, 196, 197–203
subway *(métro)*, 209–219
summer vacation *(Congé Annuel)*, 28,
    76–92
sun, 17–18, 20–21, 83–84, 90–91
surrealism, 182, 217, 228, 243–244,
    257, 266, 268–278, 297, 307–322
swingers, 192, 197
symbolism, 301

Talleyrand, Charles Maurice de, 39
Tanguy, Yves, 271
Taris, Jean, 136–138
tartine, 151, 154–164
Tavernier, Bertrand, 70–71
television, 118
"Les Temps des Cerises" ("The Time
    of Cherries"), 232, 233
terrace gardens, 240–243
Théâtre de l'Odéon, 30, 73–75, 96, 316
Thiollière, Raymond, 235, 236
Thomas, Dylan, 282, 309

Three Stories and Ten Poems
(Hemingway), 8
Through the Looking-Glass (Carroll),
103
Thurber, James, 265
tides, 87–89
Tiel, Vicky, 14–16
Tour d'Argent, 127–128
Tournon (café), 42–44, 317
Tovaritch (Deval), 135–138
Train Bleu (film), 197–198
transgender surgery, 43–44
Travels with a Donkey in the Cévennes
(Stevenson), 28–29
Trocchi, Alexander, 42
Tropic of Cancer (H. Miller), 255
La Truffière, 150–151
truffles, 150
Turin, Luca, 225
Two or Three Things I Know About Her
(film), 214
Tzara, Tristan, 271, 312

Ulysses (Joyce), 8, 22, 189, 283

Vadim, Roger, 181, 201
Vep, Irma, 275
Versailles, 28, 127–128, 157, 221
Vert-Galant, 246–249
vespasienne, pissoir, 98–102
Vian, Boris, 162–163
La Vie Sexuelle de Catherine M.
(Millet), 184–185
Vigo, Jean, 137–138
Villon, François, 74, 177–178
vintage clothing, 170–171, 173–174
Voice of America radio, 65–66
Voltaire, 156, 240, 242
Voltaire (café), 30
Voyage to the End of the Night (Céline),
136

Wagner, Richard, 7
waiters, 294–296, 317
walking, 26–33
  la griffe, 32–33, 35–36
  horseback riding *versus*, 97–98
  literary walks, 5–8 (*See also* night
  walks)
"The Waste Land" (Eliot), 217
Welsh rarebit, 157–159
Wepler (café), 42
Wescott, Glenway, 7
West, Mae, 22, 202
Wharton, Edith, 116
What's New Pussycat? (film), 11–16,
198–199
White, E. B., 55
White, Edmund, 40–41, 172–173
Williams, William Carlos, 306
Wind in the Willows, The (Grahame),
250–251
woodcuts, 235, 236, 288
word jazz/automatic writing, 277–278,
310–312
Work of Art in the Age of Mechanical
Reproduction, The (Benjamin),
185–187
World War I, 67–68, 157, 250–251,
259, 262
World War II, 18–20, 68, 90, 168,
259, 288
Wright, Richard, 42–43

X-Rated Critics Organization, 190

Yeats, W. B., 24
Young, Lester, 70

Zilahy, Iréne, 136
Zizim, Prince, 36
Zola, Émile, 124

John Baxter has lived in Paris for more than twenty years. He is the author of four acclaimed memoirs about his life in France: *The Perfect Meal: In Search of the Lost Tastes of France*; *The Most Beautiful Walk in the World: A Pedestrian in Paris*; *Immoveable Feast: A Paris Christmas*; and *We'll Always Have Paris: Sex and Love in the City of Light*. Baxter, who gives literary walking tours through Paris, is also a film critic and biographer whose subjects have included the directors Fellini, Kubrick, Woody Allen, and most recently, Josef von Sternberg. Born in Australia, he lives with his wife and daughter in the Saint-Germain-des-Prés neighborhood, in the same building Sylvia Beach called home.

BOOKS BY JOHN BAXTER

THE PERFECT MEAL
Available in Paperback and eBook

IACP COOKBOOK AWARD WINNER (*Culinary Travel*)

"Full of humor, insight, and mouth-watering details, *The Perfect Meal* is a delightful tour of 'traditional' French culture and cuisine." —*Travel + Leisure*

THE MOST BEAUTIFUL WALK IN THE WORLD
A Pedestrian in Paris

Available in Paperback and eBook

NATIONAL BESTSELLER

Baxter reveals the most beautiful walks through Paris, including the favorite routes of artists and writers who have called the city home.

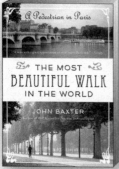

IMMOVEABLE FEAST
A Paris Christmas

Available in Paperback and eBook

The charming, funny, and improbable tale of how a man who was raised on white bread—and didn't speak a word of French—ended up preparing the annual Christmas dinner for a venerable Parisian family.

WE'LL ALWAYS HAVE PARIS
Sex and Love in the City of Light

Available in Paperback and eBook

"A charming insider's guide to literary and artistic Paris. . . . Excellent." —*Daily Mail* (London)

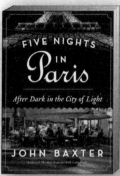

FIVE NIGHTS IN PARIS
After Dark in the City of Light
Available in Paperback and eBook

John Baxter enchanted readers with his literary tour of Paris in *The Most Beautiful Walk in the World*. Now, this expat who has lived in the City of Light for more than twenty years introduces you to the city's streets after dark, revealing hidden treasures and unexpected delights as he takes you through five of the city's greatest neighborhoods.

PARIS AT THE END OF THE WORLD
The City of Light During the Great War, 1914-1918
Available in Paperback and eBook

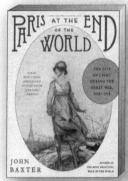

John Baxter brings to life one of the most dramatic and fascinating periods in Paris's history. As World War I ravaged France, the City of Light blazed more brightly than ever. Despite the terrifying sounds that could be heard from the capital, Parisians lived with urgency and without inhibition. The rich hosted wild parties, artists such as Picasso reached new heights, and the war brought a wave of foreigners, including Ernest Hemingway, to Paris for the first time. In this brilliant book, Baxter shows how the Great War forged the spirit of the city we love today.

CARNAL KNOWLEDGE
Baxter's Concise Encyclopedia of Modern Sex
Available in Paperback and eBook

A veritable smorgasbord of sin, John Baxter's *Carnal Knowledge* is a delightfully unabashed education in sex and erotic culture. Would you ever consent to a knee-trembler at a love hotel? Would you enjoy a hot lunch while watching kinbaku? Would you consider wearing a French tickler, a merkin, a strap-on, or pasties . . . or would you rather just go commando at the Mine Shaft? From *Deep Throat* to *Debbie Does Dallas*, from the mile-high club to the Emperor's Club, John Baxter explains it all to you in this decadently definitive work.